Backstabbers, Crazed Geniuses, and Animals We Hate

OTHER SLATE TITLES FROM ATLAS BOOKS

The Wall Street Self-Defense Manual: A Guide for the Intelligent Investor
by Henry Blodget

The Best of Slate: A 10th Anniversary Anthology

Backstabbers, Crazed Geniuses, and Animals We Hate

The Writers of *Slate*'s "Assessment" Column Tell It Like It Is

Edited by **DAVID PLOTZ**

New York

Atlas Books, LLC
10 E. 53rd St., 35th Fl.
New York NY 10022

www.atlasbooks.net

Designed by Jeff Williams

Library of Congress Cataloging-in-Publication Data
Backstabbers, crazed geniuses, and animals we hate : The writers of Slate's "Assessment" column tell it like it is / edited by David Plotz. — 1st ed.
p. cm.
Selected articles from the online magazine Slate.
ISBN 13 978-0-9777433-1-5
ISBN 10 0-9777433-1-4
1. Popular culture—United States—Miscellanea. 2. United States—Civilization—1945–Miscellanea. 3. United States—Biography—Miscellanea. 4. United States—Civilization—Miscellanea. 5. Popular culture—Miscellanea. 6. Biography—Miscellanea. I. Plotz, David. II. Slate (Redmond, Wash.)

E169.12.B25 2006
306.0973'09045—dc22

2006014958

Printed in the United States of America

First Edition

1 2 3 4 5 6 7 8 9 10

Contents

Backstabbers

Crazed Geniuses

Animals We Hate

Dead, But Won't Go Away

Tyrants

Imaginary Friends

Introduction

BY DAVID PLOTZ

WHILE READING *Backstabbers, Crazed Geniuses, and Animals We Hate*, you may decide that *Slate* writers are a bunch of cold-hearted bastards, the kind of brutes who detest cute and furry creatures (particularly pandas), dislike children, and prefer Martha Stewart to the Dalai Lama, and Rupert Murdoch to Santa Claus.

This would be an understandable conclusion, but one that slightly missed the point. The pieces collected in *Backstabbers* represent a kind of journalistic science experiment. What happens when you write profiles that reject the basic tenets of profile writing? In the early days of *Slate,* back in the mid-'90s, our founding editor Michael Kinsley recognized that the profile was one of the most abused forms in American journalism. The typical profile writer spends a tremendous amount of time and energy arranging to observe and interview a subject. The goal is to show this subject in his or her "natural" state—Donald Trump under the hair dryer, Lindsay Lohan in the club, etc. The subject responds to this spotlight by putting on an elaborate performance, which the writer then portrays as the authentic self. The resulting profile, "encrusted with useless anecdotes" (to borrow Kinsley's phrase), usually ends up being so colored by the circumstances of its preparation as to be devoid of any insight.

So Kinsley and his successor as editor, Jacob Weisberg, have chosen a different approach for *Slate*. They prefer for us to produce profiles in the style of the "portrait" pieces that appear in British newspapers on the weekend. A *Slate* profile—or "Assessment," as we prefer to call them—is a short, sharp, and decisive character study—think *Eminent Victorians,* condensed to 1,000 words. The pieces are thoroughly researched and reported, but do not depend on quotes or access. It's rare that we ask our subjects to talk to us, and even rarer for them to agree. (One of the benefits of this unusual journalistic practice is that the writer feels none of the subconscious desire to please that follows naturally from an interview.) The *Slate* Assessor develops a point of view about his subject and cuts him down to size when warranted.

Most important, *Slate* writers are encouraged to consider that everything else written about a person may be completely wrong. If we're tackling widely beloved subjects, we try our best to ignore the fog of romantic idealization that envelops them. (Maybe Lewis & Clark *didn't* change America. Maybe Mary Matalin *isn't* a brilliant Republican strategist.) When it comes to known villains, we begin by questioning the spiteful certainties of our media colleagues. (Perhaps James Dobson *isn't* entirely sinister. Perhaps the Bush twins *aren't* selfish nitwits.) We begin as ignorant but rational skeptics. The result is a collection of unconventional profiles that may sometimes be wrong, but are rarely stupid, never credulous, and often hilarious. Sometimes doubting our assumptions leads us into absurdly contrarian positions (as with Murdoch, for instance, where we argued that he has improved journalism. Or with Harry Potter, whom we determined was a "pampered jock, patsy, [and] fraud"). And sometimes we end up reaffirming the wisdom of the crowd—Bob Dylan, for example, is as much of a genius as you think, and L. Ron Hubbard was as much of a creep.

Slate published about 400 profiles in our first decade, but we only had room for the 50 best and most durable here. A lot of great pieces had to be left on the editing floor. We excluded excellent pieces about minor characters who flirted with fame but did not sustain it (who now remembers the delightfully nutty Susan Carpenter-McMillan?). We dropped people who have done too much since our Assessment was published—who would want to read a John McCain profile from 1998? We also left out a few pieces that turned out to be monumentally, utterly wrong (e.g., the Assessment suggesting that Ahmed Chalabi would make a fine president of Iraq). We've updated pieces here and there, cutting references to now obscure news events and adding analysis of the Assessee's latest accomplishments.

Discerning reader that you are, you will have noticed from the table of contents that not all the people we have profiled are, in fact, people. When I began writing our Assessment column in 1997, the stated purpose of the assignment was to examine the most interesting person in the news of that week. But in trying to come up with subjects, I soon realized that living human beings often weren't the most interesting characters in the news. Our inclusion of nonpeople began when—in a week of desperation—I wrote about El Nino, which was then ravaging the West Coast. Once you've profiled a weather pattern, pretty much anything is fair game. *Backstabbers* includes portraits of the dead (St. Patrick) and the fictional (Tarzan). We profile a body part (the Prostate), a fish (Salmon), a place (Nevada), a store (Whole Foods), and even a month (August). Dead people and nonpeople can be just as important, complicated, maddening, and lovable as living human beings. And you feel much less guilty about not trying to interview them.

BACKSTABBERS

Mother Nature

Why you can't trust Mom.

BY DAVID PLOTZ

THE BORDERS AROUND THE CORNER, which would never dream of selling dirty books, stocks its register display with another kind of smut: Weather Porn. There's *Storm of the Century*, *Isaac's Storm*, *The Perfect Storm*, *When the Wind Blows*, and my favorite, *Nature on the Rampage*, a *Kama Sutra* for weather nymphos. *Nature on the Rampage*'s cover promises "Hurricanes, Droughts, Wildfires, Tornadoes, Floods, Heat Waves, Blizzards. Also Volcanoes, Earthquakes, and even Comets!" (Even comets!) Inside are titillating photos—houses bitten in half by tornadoes, cars swallowed in snow banks, etc.—and details to arouse even the most jaded weather fetishist. Did you know that several Americans are killed every year when lightning strikes a phone pole, courses through the phone line, and electrocutes them as they are making a call? Tip: Use a cordless.

Mother Nature, the Vanessa del Rio of this weather bordello, has never seemed more fascinating than she seems today. Hollywood's flood of natural disaster movies—*Volcano*, *Twister*, *Asteroid*, *The Flood*, etc.—ebbed just in time for the real thing: the tsunami in Asia, Hurricane Katrina here. Americans have followed the natural disasters obsessively. Is there anyone who can't explain the Richter scale or distinguish between a Category 4 hurricane and a Category 5?

With all this talk of natural upheaval, you'd think we were suffering a plague of chaos—record numbers of Category 5 hurricanes, epic tornadoes, droughts, and the like. It's true that the United States, with its endless coastline, vast climatic variation, massive fault lines, and dozens of active volcanoes, is exposed to more than its share of Mother Nature's fury. But the number of natural "events" nationwide and worldwide remains constant. Some meteorologists speculate that we are entering a busy hurricane cycle, and there are worries that global warming will increase the intensity of bad weather, but the jury is still out.

Americans are more alert to Mother Nature's rage in part because more people are in its way. Half of Americans live in regions threatened by hurricanes. Earthquakes, floods, and volcanoes endanger millions more. Because property follows people, natural disasters have become more destructive: A storm that rips through Florida today shreds many more houses than it would have in 1970. According to a pre-Katrina National Science Foundation report, natural disasters now cause about $100 in damage per American per year, five times as much as a generation ago, even accounting for inflation.

But there are less tangible reasons why natural disasters obsess us. Weather is a form of war, God's conflict with man. Weather is defined by martial metaphors—"fronts," "clashing" air masses, "striking" storms. (War, curiously, is full of meteorological metaphors: a "hail" of bullets, the "fog" of battle.) Even in an age of Al Qaida and Iraq, weather narratives remain compelling war stories.

Today's paranoia about the Earth Mama also owes something to millenarianism, both religious and environmental. Christian millennial Web pages find biblical significance in every blizzard or quake. Pat Robertson thinks Disney's hospitality to gays is putting Orlando at risk. Greeniacs, too, view natural disasters as retribution. *Hot Zone* author Richard Preston, the Alfred Hitchcock of germ terror, has described murderous jungle viruses this way: "The Earth is mounting an immune response against the human species. . . . Mother Nature is going to get even."

Gaia theorists, who contend that the planet is a super-organism in which creatures unconsciously regulate the atmosphere in order to ensure favorable conditions for life, also believe Mother Nature is on the warpath. James Lovelock, who proposed the Gaia theory, writes that "Gaia . . . always keep[s] the world warm and comfortable for those who obey the rules, but [is] ruthless in her destruction of those who transgress. Her goal is a planet fit for life. If humans stand in the way of this, we shall be eliminated."

The media is another important reason Mother Nature seems more capricious these days. The ascendance of the Weather Channel, the *USA Today* weather page, and weather Web sites have turned weather into national entertainment. We can (and do) view weather satellite photos of any spot on Earth with a click, hear forecasts 24/7, and watch live footage of weather disasters on television. There is an endless appetite for weather. It is more important than sports, more dramatic than the news, and always changing.

(The media fuel weather obsession partly because we can now do something about the weather, not just talk about it. TV stations send barrages of warnings about storms, hurricanes, tornadoes, floods, blizzards. These warnings undoubtedly save lives: Natural disasters may cause more property damage in the United States, but they kill fewer people.)

The final reason for our Mother Nature obsession is politics. A primary function of any disaster is to funnel pork to important states. The president choppers in for commiseration and photo ops. The woebegone victims congratulate themselves for their fortitude. The National Guard is called out to do whatever it does (guard?). Congress busts the budget caps to protect the poor sodden folk. Then the victims bank the cash and return to their flood plain or tornado alley. Economists call this moral hazard. Politicians call it constituent service. In the end, it seems, Mother Nature is just another welfare mom, ruining homes and taking billions of tax dollars to do it.

James Dobson

The religious right's new kingmaker.

BY MICHAEL CROWLEY

ALTHOUGH THE NOTION that the religious right's "moral values" determined the 2004 election has been roundly debunked, perception is reality in politics—and the indelible perception in Washington is that, for good and for ill, George W. Bush and the Republican Party owe their evangelical Christian base big-time.

One corollary to this idea is that no one has helped Republicans win more than Dr. James Dobson. Forget Jerry Falwell and Pat Robertson, who in their dotage have marginalized themselves with gaffes (calling for assassinations of world leaders, blaming bad weather on gays, etc.). Forget Ralph Reed, dirtied by the Abramoff scandal and his lobbying career. (And forget Reed's once mighty Christian Coalition, a shell of its former self.) Forget Gary Bauer, now known chiefly as a failed presidential candidate who tumbled off a stage while flipping pancakes. Dobson is now America's most influential evangelical leader, with a following reportedly greater than that of either Falwell or Robertson at his peak.

Dobson earned the title. He proselytized hard for Bush in 2004, organizing huge stadium rallies and using his radio program to warn his 7 million American listeners that not to vote would be a sin. Dobson may have delivered Bush his victories in Ohio and Florida.

He wasted no time in leveraging his new power. When a thank-you call came from the White House, Dobson issued the staffer a blunt warning that Bush "needs to be more aggressive" about pressing the religious right's pro-life, anti–gay rights agenda, or the Republican party would "pay a price in four years." And when the pro-choice Pennsylvania Sen. Arlen Specter made conciliatory noises about appointing moderates to the Supreme Court, Dobson launched a fevered campaign to prevent him from assuming the chairmanship of the Senate Judiciary Committee. Specter was allowed to keep the chair only after kowtowing to conservatives.

As newly powerful figures are wont to do, Dobson overplayed his hand. When Harriet Miers was nominated to the Supreme Court, Dobson quickly vouched for her credentials as a religious conservative. (Karl Rove, knowing of Dobson's influence, had called him to ask for his support and to assure him of Miers' soundness.) Dobson's endorsement backfired when it turned out that Miers' record suggested she was less socially conservative than Dobson claimed. Her withdrawal as a nominee embarrassed and chastened Dobson.

But he remains a conservative kingmaker, which, surprisingly, isn't a role he's traditionally sought or relished (and may relish even less post-Miers). An absolutist disgusted by the compromises of politics, he sneers at those who place "self-preservation and power ahead of moral principle." He has always kept his distance from Washington. Unlike Reed, a canny strategist above all, Dobson has talked about bringing down the GOP if it fails him. Yet as the gay-marriage movement surged this year, Dobson's moral outrage over the direction of American culture went supernova, asserting in his recent book *Marriage Under Fire* that Western civilization hangs in the balance. Dobson now faces a difficult trial. He must decide which he hates more, Washington politics or cultural apocalypse.

Dobson's clout emanates from Focus on the Family, a Colorado Springs–based ministry he founded that is awesome in scope: publishing books and magazines, disseminating Dobson's weekly newspaper column to more than 500 papers, and airing radio shows—including Dobson's own—that reach people in 115 countries every week, from Japan to Botswana and in languages from Spanish to Zulu. The ministry receives so much mail it has its own ZIP code.

His rise began in 1977, when as an unknown pediatric psychologist in California he published *Dare to Discipline*, a denunciation of permissive parenting that tried to rehabilitate the practice of spanking. The book sold 2 million copies. Dobson then cranked out a string of follow-up Christian self-help books, with titles like *Straight Talk to Men* and *What Wives Wish Their Husbands Knew About Women*.

What made Dobson's books successful wasn't, as you might think, bilious jeremiads about modernity, but rather their highly practical advice about daily challenges from midlife crises to sibling rivalry. In these books and elsewhere, Dobson can sound like a perfectly sensible, if conservative, pop psychologist, not too different from Dr. Phil. On his Web site, he replies to a query about a marriage stuck in the doldrums. Instead of haranguing the questioner about the covenant of marriage, Dobson concedes that "adults still love the thrill of the chase, the lure of the unattainable, the excitement of the new and boredom with the old. Immature impulses are controlled and minimized in a committed relationship, of course, but they never fully disappear."

Possessed of a friendly, fatherly manner, Dobson can even play the part of genial cornball. A passage in *Straight Talk to Men*, for instance, meant to show Dobson's sympathy for ordinary families, recounts what he calls "the day we now refer to as 'Black Sunday.'" On that gruesome morning, it turns out, the Dobsons woke up late for church, spilled some milk at breakfast and—Lord have mercy!—lost their tempers after a Dobson child got his church clothes dirty. "At least one spanking was delivered, as I recall, and another three or four were promised. Yes, it was a day to be remembered (or forgotten)," Dobson writes. The lament sounds like something you'd hear from the hyper-geeky and ultra-devout Ned Flanders of *The Simpsons*.

Initially, Dobson indeed focused on the family, keeping his distance (as many evangelicals customarily did) from the political arena's dirty deal-making. But as his following grew, he warmed to politics. In 1983 he established the Family Research Council as his political arm, although he dispatched his friend Gary Bauer to the Council's office in the Gomorrah of Washington so Dobson could concentrate on his ministry in Colorado. Then, in the late 1990s Dobson began to grow disenchanted with Republican leaders in Congress for not pushing the Christian social agenda harder. In the 2000 campaign his tepid support of Bush may have helped dampen turnout among evangelical voters, a disappointment Karl Rove dwelled on for four years.

It was the gay-marriage debate that finally hurled Dobson into politics wholeheartedly. The subject of homosexuality seems to exert a special power over him, and he has devoted much idiosyncratic thought to it. When discussing gays he spares no detail, no matter how prurient. In *Bringing Up Boys*, he gleefully reprints a letter he received from a 13-year-old boy who describes wiggling his naked body in front of the mirror to "make my genitals bounce up and down" and admits to having "tried more than once to suck my own penis (to be frank)." Dobson believes that such adolescents suffer from what he calls "pre-homosexuality," a formative stage that results from having a weak father figure. Dobson further contends that homosexuality, especially in such an early stage, can be "cured." His ministry runs a program called Love Won Out that seeks to convert "ex-gays" to heterosexuality. (Alas, the program's director, a self-proclaimed "ex-gay" himself, was spotted at a gay bar in 2000, an episode Dobson downplayed as "a momentary setback.")

To Dobson, gay marriage is a looming catastrophe of epic proportions. He has compared the recent steps toward gay marriage to Pearl Harbor and likens the battle against it to D-Day. While

Dobson maintains that he'd prefer to stay out of politics, he has said that "the attack and assault on marriage is so distressing that I just feel like I can't remain silent." In 2004, Dobson started a new offshoot of Focus on the Family called Focus on the Family Action, which he used to campaign openly for Bush. And during the campaign he joined Ralph Reed and born-again Watergate conspirator Charles Colson in regular conference calls with Karl Rove and other senior White House officials.

Dobson won a major battle with Bush's reelection. But success brings its own perils (again, see: Miers, Harriet). It's quite possible that Dobson, his hopes having been raised, will find them dashed. After all, Republican strategists surely realize that too strong an antigay stand could further alienate moderates and independents.

Perhaps more damaging is the possibility that Dobson gets what he wants. Maybe the GOP will establish an anti-abortion Supreme Court, overturn *Roe v. Wade*, stamp out gay rights, ban stem-cell research forever, and shut down MTV and cancel *The Bachelor*. Voters may not be so pleased with the Republican Party after that. Despite the qualms they showed about gay marriage this year, there's no reason to think they want anything like Dobson's Utopia, and they could see a replay of, say, 1998, when the perception that angry culture warriors were running the GOP damaged the party at the polls. In one of his books, Dobson has written of the gay-rights movement that "evil has a way of overreaching." So does the far right.

Michiko Kakutani

A critic with a fixation.

BY BEN YAGODA

MICHIKO KAKUTANI RECENTLY EMBARKED on her 25th year as a *New York Times* book critic, and it's gotten to the point that when her name is mentioned in print, you can see the smoke rising from the page. The late Susan Sontag complained, "Her criticisms of my books are stupid and shallow and not to the point." Salman Rushdie referred to her as "a weird woman who seems to feel the need to alternately praise and spank." Most notoriously, in 2005 Norman Mailer called Kakutani, who is of Japanese descent, a "one-woman kamikaze" and a "token" minority hire.

Those who rip her are usually authors she has ripped, and their indignation often muddies their logic. Certainly Mailer's insinuations, in addition to being boorish, are unsupportable. It should be clear to anyone who has read Kakutani's reviews that she has an estimable intelligence; she backs this up with what must be many real or virtual all-nighters in which she digests every word ever published by the writer under review. She takes books seriously, a valuable and ever-rarer trait. Furthermore, in my observation, she is more or less right in her judgments most of the time. (I slightly knew Kakutani when we were undergraduates at Yale about 30 years ago but have not spoken to her since.)

But the sour-grapes sniping from spurned authors should not obscure the fact that Kakutani is a profoundly uninteresting critic. Her main weakness is her evaluation fixation. This may seem an odd complaint—the job is called critic, after all—but in fact, whether a work is good or bad is just one of the many things to be said about it, and usually far from the most important or compelling. Great critics' bad calls are retrospectively forgiven or ignored: Pauline Kael is still read with pleasure even though no one still agrees (if anyone ever did) that *Last Tango in Paris* and *Nashville* are the cinematic equivalents of "The Rite of Spring" and *Anna Karenina*. Kakutani doesn't offer the stylistic flair, the wit, or the insight one gets from Kael and other first-rate critics; for her, the verdict is the only thing. One has the sense of her deciding roughly at page 2 whether or not a book is worthy; reading the rest of it to gather evidence for her case; spending some quality time with the thesaurus; and then taking a large blunt hammer and pounding the message home.

That message is harsh an awful lot of the time, and publishing folk commonly complain that Kakutani is too hard to please. It's true that the pleasure she appears to take in hurling a voluminous stream of harsh epithets at each dead horse is a bit unseemly, and that her perennial frustration with writers gives her a prim, schoolmarmish air. But negativity has been a good career strategy for her: The citation on her 1998 Pulitzer Prize gave props to her "fearless and authoritative" judgments. And the bigger problem, once again, isn't the number or severity of the pans but the pan-rave mentality. She sometimes seems to be channeling Matthew Arnold, a titan of literature but not the best role model for a newspaper book critic. Arnold was the solemn Victorian who defined criticism as "the disinterested endeavor to learn and propagate the best that is known and thought in the world" and believed "its business is to do this with inflexible honesty." Arnold compared every work that came across his desk to the "touchstones" that represented the highest standards. If something lacked "high seriousness" (as he felt of Chaucer's and Robert Burns' poetry), it got the inflexible honesty treatment.

Kakutani started her career as a reporter, and her reviews usually have a who-what-when-where news lede right up top that sums up the verdict. In the second paragraph of her review of Nick Hornby's latest novel, she calls it a "maudlin bit of tripe. 'A Long Way Down' is utterly devoid of the wonderfully acute observations of pop culture that made the author's debut novel, 'High Fidelity' (1995), such a rollicking delight to read, and it is equally devoid of the sorts of savvy social and psychological insights that fueled his impassioned soccer memoir, 'Fever Pitch' (1994). Instead, this cringe-making excuse for a novel takes the sappy contrivances of his 2001 book, 'How to Be Good,' to an embarrassing new low."

I've read *A Long Way Down*, so let me use it and the passage just quoted as a case study of Kakutani's problems as a writer. The novel is far from "a rollicking delight." (That phrase, by the way, is an example of how Kakutani's prose is even flatter when it praises than when it buries.) But a list of deficiencies, and a bit of plot summary, is all Kakutani has for us, and, lacking any other ideas or themes, she (characteristically) exaggerates the novel's faults. In her world, books tend to be masterpieces or rubbish; in the real one, they're almost always somewhere in between. She also (characteristically) sets up a bogus dichotomy between *A Long Way Down* and the "good" Hornby books. In fact, an artist's works almost always have more similarities than differences; if the disjuncture here were really as big as she claims, it should be the main subject of her review. The core question is how the current piece fits into the oeuvre, and we expect reflective reviews to address it. In this case, I'd be curious to see a critic consider Hornby's oft-stated and almost obsessive pledge to write books that are entertaining and ultimately uplifting—and how such a project could be expected eventually to encounter artistic and philosophical difficulties.

You'd want this Platonic critic to touch on other stuff, too. He or she could share some insights about the nature of novels written in dramatic monologues, or novels about suicide, or novels, or art, or life. Kakutani's refusal ever to take her eyes off the thumbs up/thumbs down prize, or to lay any of her own prejudices, tastes, or tangentially relevant observations on the table, is dispiriting. One of her favorite gimmicks for ducking subjectivity is to invoke the supposed reactions of "the reader" to a book. This is a rather underhanded device with a tweedy scent of 1940s and '50s arbiters like Lionel Trilling and Clifton Fadiman—and it's a perfect emblem of the way Kakutani muffles her own voice by hiding behind a mask. But it provides the only fun I get from her reviews: First thing, I always hunt for "the reader" (whom I visualize as a kind of miniature androgynous Michelin man) the way I used to count the Ninas in a Hirschfeld drawing. Imagine my delight to come upon Kakutani's January review of Richard Reeves' *President Reagan* and find two successive sentences telling us that "the reader turns in eager anticipation" to the book because Reeves' previous works on Kennedy and Nixon gave "the reader minutely detailed accounts" of their presidencies.

As a student at Oxford, the future drama critic Kenneth Tynan got back a paper with this comment: "Keep a strict eye on eulogistic & dyslogistic adjectives—They shd diagnose (not merely blame) & distinguish (not merely praise.)" Tynan's tutor, who happened to be C.S. Lewis, was offering a lesson Kakutani could have benefited from. "Utterly devoid . . . wonderfully acute observations . . . debut novel . . . savvy social and psychological insights . . . cringe-making . . . embarrassing new low": Virtually every word or phrase is a cliché, or at best shopworn and lifeless, and evidence of Kakutani's solid tin ear. (She has justly been called out for her near-obsessive use of "lugubrious" and "limn," words that probably have never been said aloud in the history of English.) That's what can happen to a writer when she merely praises and merely blames. Kakutani appears incapable of engaging with language, either playfully or seriously, which puts her at a painful disadvantage when she is supposed to be evaluating writers who can and do. Here, she tries to energize the prose with lapel-grabbing intensifiers like utterly and wonderfully and superfluous adjectives like savvy and embarrassing, but they just make her look like she's protesting too much. (Another Lewis quote with relevance to Kakutani: "If we are not careful criticism may become a mere excuse for taking revenge on books whose smell we dislike by erecting our temperamental antipathies into pseudo-moral judgments.")

The qualities most glaringly missing from Kakutani's work are humor and wit. Maybe in an attempt to compensate, she writes one or two parody reviews a year: of a book about swinging London in the voice of Austin Powers, of a Bridget Jones book in the voice of Ally McBeal, of Benjamin Kunkel's novel *Indecision* in the voice of Holden Caulfield, of Truman Capote's recently discovered novella in the voice of Holly Golightly. Talk about cringemaking. They are so awful, from start to finish, that you cannot avert your eyes, much as you would like to.

The voice this reader would really like to hear in Michiko Kakutani's reviews is not a mock–Holly Golightly voice or the enervated (or prissy) voice of an enshrined critic, but Kakutani's own. Here's a modest suggestion on how to start: Just once, instead of describing what "the reader" expects, thinks, or does, she might try using the word "I."

Lobbyists

There are two kinds, Swindlers and Fixers. Which is worse?

BY JACOB WEISBERG

THERE ARE VASTLY MORE LOBBYISTS in Washington than ever before, but understanding them remains relatively simple. There are two basic types: the swindlers and the fixers.

The swindler is represented by Jack Abramoff, who got Indian tribes to pay him millions of dollars to help legalize casinos on their reservations, and then pay him more millions to protect them from potential competitors who, as it happens, were also paying Abramoff millions to legalize their gambling operations. That Abramoff, an Orthodox Jew, had the bright idea of enlisting fundamentalist Christians to assist his Indians gives the scandal a delightful *Blazing Saddles* quality.

In Washington, the swindler's native habitat is the golf course and the stadium skybox, where he woos his clients and refreshes his relationships to people with power. A carnivore, he lives on a diet of steak, cabernet sauvignon, and cheesecake, served in excessive portions in the brass-and-leather "power" restaurant that he owns or is at least a partner in. The swindler spends a great deal of time prowling fund-raisers and receptions in order to be seen and photographed with his arm around elected officials. He cultivates a naughty image and does not mind being criticized in the press for being an "influence peddler," which only proves that he has influence to peddle. Short of a criminal investigation, infamy is free advertising.

The swindler lobbyist's natural prey is the naive but cynical client—the African dictator, the Russian oligarch, or the casino Indian, who thinks the game in Washington is rigged and that he must pay someone like Abramoff to play and win it. Such clients take the swindler's boasts about his connections and his ability to make things happen at face value. They don't ask questions when he suggests, for instance, that the way to keep the Mariana Islands exempt from labor laws is to give half a million dollars to something called the U.S. Family Network or to contribute to a think tank that underwrites golf junkets. The swindler may or may not do anything that actually helps his clueless clients, who don't understand the true value of having something inserted in the *Congressional Record*: precisely nil.

The lobbyist-as-fixer is epitomized by the late gray eminence Clark Clifford, who served several presidents beginning with Harry Truman and "advised" corporations on how to get what they wanted from the government, before being brought low by the BCCI banking scandal at the end of his career. According to legend, the elegant, silver-haired Clifford would greet every new customer by saying he had no influence and would not go to see the president on a client's behalf (wink, wink). The fixer is almost always a lawyer and recoils at even being called a lobbyist.

The fixer styles himself in opposition to the swindler. His habitat is the Georgetown drawing room or the Metropolitan Club, where he retells his well-worn anecdotes about LBJ and Richard Nixon, not Tom DeLay. He doesn't socialize promiscuously or revel in the high life. His work takes place over the phone or in boring, substantive meetings. The fixer is the soul of discretion and would never drop the names of clients, with whom he cultivates decades-long relationships. What, if anything, he accomplishes for them remains largely a mystery, since neither he nor they want you to know.

Leading Washington fixers have been quoted in the press in recent days trying to explain that what they do is categorically different from what Abramoff was up to. He was gauche and corrupt; they do dignified work protected by the Constitution. In fact, the differences between fixers and swindlers are mostly cosmetic and irrelevant from the point of view of the public interest.

In economic terms, hired-gun lobbyists of all varieties engage in "rent-seeking"—finding a way to rake off a share of someone else's profits by interposing themselves in what ought to be open processes of democratic decision-making. In so doing, they make everyone poorer, except perhaps cigar sellers and suppliers of prime beef to Washington restaurants. In a way, the fixers are worse than the swindlers because they are likely to be more effective at inserting indecipherable little clauses into legislation that result in more government spending or reduced tax revenue.

To be sure, private and organized interests have every right to press their cases with lawmakers and regulators. But mercenary lobbyists, who sell influence that has usually been acquired through past work in government, are doing something inherently disreputable. Professional lobbyists exploit relationships and knowledge they developed as public servants for the purpose of enriching themselves. What they do may be technically legal, but it is nonetheless corrupt, because it's an exchange (if not a specific transaction) of campaign contributions and other goodies for special treatment in the legislative process.

Until the Abramoff scandal, the party that ran Washington openly celebrated the lobbying industry, regarding it as a branch of its endless patronage empire and a kind of Fifth Estate. Now even Republican congressmen who were planning to one day become lobbyists will feel compelled to vote for tighter restrictions, such as longer waiting periods before they can lobby their old colleagues and more stringent disclosure laws. But such reforms will mean very little unless professional lobbying comes to be regarded once again as a shady and shameful activity rather than the quickest way to get rich if you happen to lose an election.

The Prostate

Why the gland is so famous.

BY DAVID PLOTZ

JUST A FEW YEARS AGO, newspapers were declaring prostate cancer the "hush-hush man-killer," "the silent enemy," and "the disease that dare not speak its name." Then everyone started blabbing about their prostate. New York Mayor Rudolph Giuliani held a press conference to announce his prostate cancer. Intel CEO Andy Grove took the cover of *Fortune* to chronicle his struggle against the disease. Joe Torre's prostate helped spur the New York Yankees to a World Series title. Gen. Norman Schwarzkopf can't stop talking about his gland. Larry King devoted an entire show to the prostate—an hour that included Sam Donaldson describing how he examined his groin in the shower and King urging his male viewers to get a prostate exam, the "old-fashioned digital, the finger in the rectum."

The disease that dare not speak its name has become the disease that won't shut up.

Breast cancer remains a cause célèbre, Lance Armstrong gave testicular cancer a brief shining moment, and the colon—sponsored by Katie Couric—is making headlines, but prostate cancer has become America's favorite malignancy, Cancer Enemy No. 1. The number of articles about the prostate has quintupled in the past five years. Research funding has quadrupled. You can't turn around without bumping into a famous prostate cancer survivor (Marion Barry, Sidney Poitier, Bob Dole . . .)

But why should the nasty little gland be so trendy? The prostate, after all, has always been with us, and it's still doing the same tedious work. A gland the size of a walnut wrapped around the urethra, it hangs just below the bladder, in front of the rectum, and above the penis. It has one important job: It produces seminal fluid ejaculated during orgasm. That fluid nourishes sperm on their journey to the egg.

Perhaps because its cells divide frequently, the prostate is prone to malignancy. About 180,000 American men are diagnosed with prostate cancer every year, and more than 30,000 die of it. After lung cancer, it is the deadliest cancer for American men, killing three out of 100.

Prostate cancer is capturing the popular imagination partly because there is more of it. Prostate cancer diagnoses doubled in the United States from the mid-'70s to the mid-'90s. The graying of the population explains some of this increase. American men are living longer, and almost every man who lives long enough develops prostate problems. The overwhelming majority of American men who reach 80 suffer from benign prostatic hyperplasia, an expansion of the prostate that causes urinary discomfort. And most men who live long enough also suffer from prostate cancer. According to an American Cancer Society book, one-third of men in their 40s have prostate cancer—usually too small and too slow-growing to notice—while 80 percent of men in their 80s have it.

Aggressive screening also helps explain the increase. The key diagnostic test, the PSA, has been commonly used only since the late '80s. The American Cancer Society recommends that men begin annual prostate tests at age 50. African-Americans, whose prostate cancer rate is double that of whites, should begin at 40 or 45, as should men with a family history of prostate cancer. (Men in the United States, perhaps because of diet, have the highest prostate cancer rates in the world. Men in Asia have the lowest.)

Prostate cancer is a satisfying target because it is eminently curable. Prostate cancer death rates have dropped 16 percent in the '90s. If cancer has not spread beyond the prostate, surgical removal of the prostate is nearly 100 percent successful. Radiation therapy is almost as effective, curing more than 80 percent of patients and causing fewer side effects. When cancer has spread beyond the prostate, treatment is more drastic. Doctors must reduce testosterone levels to starve the tumors. This requires either antiandrogen drugs or surgical castration, both of which destroy the sex drive.

Despite their success fighting prostate cancer, doctors disagree vehemently about whether men should be tested routinely. Prostate cancer is generally slow-moving and dim-witted. Even left untreated, it does not kill most of the people who have it: In most cases, the malignancy confines itself to the prostate and causes few if any symptoms. (Oncologists like to say that you are more likely to die with prostate cancer than of prostate cancer.) The slow growth of most prostate tumors means that many patients diagnosed with prostate cancer will never be bothered by the disease. But, understandably, few patients risk refusing treatment once they know they have cancer.

This poses a dilemma, because prostate cancer treatment has terrible side effects. Surgery leaves many patients impotent and a significant percentage incontinent. Radiation frequently causes impotence and bowel problems. As a result, some medical organizations, including the National Cancer Institute, do not recommend routine prostate testing. They argue that it leads to harmful treatment of many men who would otherwise never be bothered by their slow-growing cancer. The American Cancer Society, which does favor testing, counters that not testing endangers men with fast-growing cancer. Their tumors may not be discovered till too late. The ACS also notes that improved surgical techniques are making side effects less heinous: Some surgeons claim that less than 20 percent of their patients suffer impotence and less than 5 percent suffer incontinence. (Most oncologists and surgeons agree that men whose life expectancy is less than 10 years should not undergo surgery or radiation. The therapies are too destructive, and the patients are more likely to die from other causes than from their untreated cancer.)

Prostate cancer is also benefiting from a vigorous public-relations campaign spearheaded by Michael Milken. The former junk-bond dealer was diagnosed with serious prostate cancer as soon as he came out of prison in 1993. After successful treatment, he threw himself into prostate promotion, doing for prostate cancer what breast cancer victims did for their disease. He endowed a foundation, CapCURE, to fund research. He and other prostate cancer victims have lobbied Congress and the National Cancer Institute to boost government funding for prostate research. The NCI has hiked prostate funding massively, though it still lags far behind NCI's budget for breast cancer, which kills about the same number of people. The prostate campaigners have persuaded famous men to go public about the prostate, enlisting Arnold Palmer and Harry Belafonte to discuss their glands and George Foreman to pose for "Real men get it checked" ads.

The psycho-sexual anxiety of boomers fuels prostate-mania. Boomer men are entering their peak prostate cancer years. Many have just passed the 50-year mark, and the rest are rapidly approaching it. They're already paranoid about preserving their health and vitality. Prostate cancer terrifies boomers because it so threatens sexual potency. Prostate cancer negates masculinity. It leaves healthy men impotent and incontinent. It unmans. Is it any wonder boomers obsess over it?

Above all, the prostate craze represents a rare triumph for America's culture of shamelessness. Men didn't talk about their prostates a generation ago: It was unseemly and embarrassing. Thousands of men avoided treatment and probably died because of it. But now reticence is passé. The president's sex organs are analyzed in public, sex therapy occurs in prime time, no one blinks at nudity, profanity, or violence. This culture of blab and revelation—otherwise so icky—mercifully airs out the prostate closet. Not talking about the prostate killed men. Talking about it—in the most graphic terms—scares men, sends them to the doctor, and gets them treated. It is surely awkward to watch Larry King rapture over his rectal exams. Just remember that his ass may be saving someone else's.

Mary Matalin

The virtues of failing upward.

BY ANDREW FERGUSON

FAILING UPWARD IS A COMMON FORM of getting ahead in certain corners of corporate America, but nowhere is the method as sure-fire as it is in Washington. Many of the capital's most recognizable personages sashay through town trailing a long history of fuck-ups. Think of Oliver North, whose idiocy and ineptitude almost destroyed the administration he worked for and who received, as compensation, a nightly TV show and five-figure speaking fees; or Warren Christopher, whose bungling of the Iranian hostage crisis under President Carter catapulted him to the job of secretary of state in the next Democratic administration; or think of the Monster of the Mess-Up, the Icon of Incompetence, the Big Bopper of the Blooper, Robert McNamara, whose achievements include not only blood-soaked rice paddies in Vietnam but also, and almost as bad, the Edsel. For this he was awarded the presidency of the World Bank, and we honor him still.

In this company of stars, Mary Matalin holds a special place. So great is her success, so large (by Washington standards) is her fame, and so unidentifiable is her talent that the rest of the capital's strivers can only gawk in wonder. Matalin first came to public attention as a lieutenant to Lee Atwater, the gifted, despicable political operative who led George Bush's successful 1988 presidential campaign and later became chairman of the Republican National Committee. Matalin served Atwater until his death from brain cancer in 1991. By then she was well connected in GOP politics, and President Bush named her political director of his reelection campaign. The choice was controversial among some Republican mossbacks. Her boyfriend at the time was James Carville, a Democratic consultant about to take over Bill Clinton's presidential campaign and easily the equal of Atwater in his manic energy and his gift for promoting himself as a talented eccentric. To appease the mossbacks, Carville and Matalin announced to colleagues and the press that they would put their romance in abeyance for the duration of the campaign.

They were fibbing. They continued to see each other in secret throughout 1992 and to trade intimacies in nightly phone calls when cruel fate kept them apart. That little bit of disloyalty aside, it is difficult to convey to normal people how touching some professional Washingtonians—those whose lives are otherwise consumed with cold-blooded political careerism—found the story of the Matalin-Carville romance. In a city built upon the will to power, this is what passes for a fairy tale come true, suggesting the transcendent nature of love itself. Mary and James proved that even people whose soul-deep obsession was party politics, the bloodier the better, could be tamed by romance.

This isn't true either. Of course, political warriors in Washington like to pretend to the ideal of comity. "We're all friends after five o'clock" was the often quoted and utterly insincere motto of Tip O'Neill. In fact Democratic and Republican true believers cleave almost exclusively to their own—as unmingled as Hutus and Tutsis, though with better table manners. Why should it be otherwise? If politics is truly the encompassing passion of your life, no one should be surprised if you seek friendship and conviviality and love (especially love) among people whose politics are similar to yours. They should be surprised if you don't. Solemnized a year after Election Day 1992 in an elaborate New Orleans wedding, the union of right-wing Mary and left-wing James thus raised an uncomfortable question. Which were they faking—the love or the politics? It would be unseemly to question their love, so let's assume the answer is politics, but with an important qualification. There are two kinds of politics. One involves the clash of dearly held ideas, a contest between defining views of the world. The other has to do with buzz and gamesmanship, tactics and maneuvering. In this second kind of politics, ideas and worldviews are mere instruments, a board game accessory, as exchangeable as Monopoly money.

By sheerest coincidence, James and Mary rose to celebrity just as cable TV was metastasizing a kind of chat show dedicated precisely to politics as they understood it. Following such '80s successes as *Crossfire* and *The McLaughlin Group*, it was the mission of *Hardball* and *Talk Back Live* and *Hannity and Colmes*—and to a lesser extent, the new *Meet the Press*, where they were soon appearing regularly—to trivialize politics into a compulsively entertaining freak show. It was a parody of idea politics. Two sharply drawn sides, conservative and liberal, sputtered across a desk, and Carville and Matalin obliged by becoming the *Battling Bickersons* of the Beltway. (Matalin herself debuted her own cable show, *Equal Time*, in 1993. She and her co-host Jane Wallace mingled semi-serious interviews with chit-chat about their troubles with cellulite, but even by the subterranean standards of cable, the show was too creepy to catch on.) By then certifiably famous, Matalin and Carville followed the career path of pure celebrity—a short-lived radio show, lucrative endorsement contracts (for Alka Seltzer, American Express), a best-selling memoir, and endless *Bickerson* performances in front of trade groups, corporate seminars, universities, and the other chumps-with-too-much-money who lubricate the nation's gab circuit. They opened a restaurant. They had a couple of kids.

All this activity serves to obscure the important question of why Matalin and Carville should have become famous at all. It's a funny thing about failing up in Washington. People who fail up here are not failures in the conventional sense; they're failures only at what they're supposed to be good at. McNamara, for example, was held to be a genius at "strategizing" (the term was new then) and organizing large bureaucracies; he failed miserably at both while excelling at the far more valuable art of bum-bussing and knowing whose bum to buss. Carville and Matalin are reputed to be crackerjack political operatives. The evidence is slim. Matalin's signature political experience was as an architect of George Bush's re-election campaign. Carville went from failure to failure as a consultant until he engineered the upset win of a Pennsylvania Senate seat, after which Bill Clinton plucked him from obscurity. In short, one of them helped design what is widely understood as the worst presidential campaign in modern memory, and the other ran against the worst presidential campaign in modern memory and managed to win only 43 percent of the vote.

Their genuine gifts are the gifts that Washington truly prizes. Chief among these is their willingness to promote themselves as easily graspable caricatures. It has brought them to the pinnacle of Washington celebrity. This is why, when Matalin agreed in 2001 to leave CNN's *Crossfire* for a gig in Dubya's White House, the move seemed like a demotion: A White House job is what one fails at while one is on his way to ever greater things—screw up there, *end up* as an analyst on CNN. No surprise, then, that she cut short her stint in Dick Cheney's press office—having made no discernible improvement in the vice president's reputation—and went back to TV. (She also runs a conservative book publishing imprint and makes occasional freelance appearances as a White House adviser, notably during the disastrous week after the vice president shot his hunting partner). This time around, though, she went on TV not as a commentator for a news network, but as a character named "Mary Matalin" on Steven Soderbergh's HBO series *K Street*. It was a perfect fit—the candidates were fictional, so she had no one to promote but herself.

CRAZED GENIUSES

Cirque du Soleil

Canada's insane clown posse.

BY BRYAN CURTIS

CIRQUE DU SOLEIL IS ONE OF THE great artistic follies of our age and one of its most baffling success stories. At a given moment, as many as four productions populate the Las Vegas Strip, while others prepare to invade Perth, Australia; Osaka, Japan; and Ostend, Belgium. Cirque du Soleil has spawned a feature film, a reality TV series, and a theater-cum-spa in Montreal. Since decamping Quebec in 1987 with a show titled *Le Cirque Réinventé* ("the circus reinvented"), it has all but banished P.T. Barnum's prehistoric sideshows from the imagination. Five years ago, in a desperate bid to reclaim their birthright, Barnum's heirs produced a knockoff of the classier Canuck show—sans midway and avec fatuousness. It flopped. Meanwhile, Cirque founder Guy Laliberté—such an inspiring name!—exudes French-Canadian benevolence. He does not say, "There's a sucker born every minute." He says, "I dream of filling the planet with creativity."

Which is not to say that Cirque du Soleil isn't a uniquely terrifying experience. Touring stateside not long ago was a show called *Varekai*, which in the Romany language means "wherever." Cirque's Web site described its setting as "an extraordinary world . . . populated by fantastical creatures." The tickets, however, directed us to the extraordinary hamlet of East Rutherford, N.J., where most of the fantastical creatures seem to have ridden the bus in from Port Authority. I arrived a few minutes late and found the stage occupied by a small goat-man with forest leaves protruding from his trousers and his hair gelled into a three-point salute. "Pfffft!" he said, to much laughter. A few moments later, an angel dressed in white descended from the heavens. The goat-man regarded the angel with mock fury until the angel rose and began to perform trapeze stunts with the aid of a hammock. This seemed to satisfy the goat-man and he departed at stage right. Then a parade of oddities: a troupe of flame-colored acrobats; children dressed in puffy suits as if they were about to train attack dogs, performing with bolas; empty-eyed ogres dressed as samurai warriors and rhythmically stomping their feet. That brought the first act to a close.

Varekai was so profoundly jarring, so uncertain in its narrative intentions, that when the lights came up nobody in the audience could think to move. At least at the end of similarly exotic occasions—like a Megadeth concert or a White House press conference—the crowd knows when to get up. A small boy sitting a few feet to my right and using a voice reserved for pre-adolescent terror turned to his mother and shrieked, "What's going *on*?!" He spoke for all of us.

Why does Cirque du Soleil endure? Amid the excitement, it seems as if Guy Laliberté has created a revolutionary new art form from scratch. This isn't quite true, and to understand Cirque, you must first understand how the American circus divided into two opposing camps. The first, exemplified by Ringling Bros. and Barnum & Bailey, consists of the robust sideshow that rumbles into town trailing clowns, a menagerie, and a thriving community of midway creeps. Spread across three rings, the performances are hectic and diffuse; the goal is to produce nonstop, and often nonsensical, wonders. In response, outfits like San Francisco's Pickle Family Circus had by the mid–1970s begun to experiment with a more artistically minded circus. They set aside the animals, reduced three rings to one, and highlighted the athletic and comic skills of the human performers. Angling for the intimacy of street performance and the Italian commedia dell'arte, the Pickles and others created modest spectacles—a "New American Circus," as it was called—that forswore chaos in favor of an emotional connection with the audience.

Viewed from this perspective, Cirque du Soleil looks less like a reinvention than a refinement—a New New American Circus, wedged between spectacle and shoestring. Cirque's founders like to boast of humble origins: The show sprang from the mind of Laliberté, then a penniless 24-year-old street-based fire-eater who pestered the Quebec government for grants to support his troupe. Today, a Cirque du Soleil performance has only one ring, and the violin remains the background instrument of choice. Yet "humble" and "intimate" are not the first words one would choose to describe Laliberté's shows, which have a Barnum-like mandate to mesmerize. *Varekai*'s set featured dozens of bamboo-like trees that performers would shimmy up and down, half-visible in the Technicolor lights. When the violin receded, merciless New Age music played wall-to-wall. As Cirque planned a Beatles-themed show in Las Vegas' Mirage Hotel next year—a show that was replacing the hotel's former occupants, Siegfried and Roy—the troupe's transformation from street performance to rock concert will be complete. This is the magic of Cirque: It's artistically pure enough to please the aesthete and yet crass enough for the Las Vegas Strip.

Crassness, of course, is one of the pleasures of the circus: You can marvel at the freaks more repulsive than yourself. Here, too, Cirque has taken Barnum's dark, crowd-pleasing impulses and refined the approach. There were all kinds of oddities on display in *Varekai*—bloated clowns, loose-limbed children—but by wrapping them in pastels and setting their movements to music, Laliberté gave them a dignity rarely afforded by the sideshow. Joel Schechter, a historian at San Francisco State University, notes that Cirque du Soleil has even lent new majesty to the contortionist. In the original run of *Varekai*, Olga Pikhienko balanced on her hands and wrapped her legs behind her head like a pretzel. In any other setting, such an act would only elicit sympathy pains in the anterior cruciate ligaments. And yet in her white bodysuit, Pikhienko had a pure, almost virginal beauty: She looked like a ballerina, a delicate Lladro statuette.

Finally, there's the matter of exoticism. A great deal of Cirque du Soleil's magic comes from its unapologetic Frenchness. Or, if you prefer, its Quebecoisity. By this, I mean that Cirque du Soleil's shows make absolutely no sense at all. I studied the plot of *Varekai* for a solid hour before attending the performance, but by the end of the second act I was blubbering the same nonsense as the goat-man. But Cirque embraces bafflement. As with acts like Blue Man Group and *De La Guarda*, its audiences relish the idea of watching something queer and foreign—it gives the impression of some unattainable highbrow culture, even if the underlying principle is nothing so much as bedlam. (Cirque motto: "Take comfort in the chaos.") As Cirque grows into a global behemoth, queerness becomes a two-way street: It reflects the cultural displacement of audience member and performer alike. In a 1990 Cirque show called *Nouvelle Expérience*, a clown stood alone on stage, clutching a suitcase and peering at the crowd as if he'd just flown in from Mars. After departing Cirque du Soleil's big top and blinking at the minivans rolling into the Jersey hinterlands, I recognized the feeling.

Antonin Scalia

The Supreme Court's pocket Jeremiah.

BY DAHLIA LITHWICK

IT'S BECOME SOMETHING OF A SPECTATOR SPORT, in recent years. First, Justice Antonin Scalia will give an intemperate speech, hunt with a named party in a pending case, or otherwise do something to suggest he's already made up his mind on some matter currently before the Supreme Court. As night follows day, calls will come for his recusal. He will usually refuse. With each successive episode one wonders whether Scalia was ever given that advice the rest of us heard as children: about counting to 10 before you do or say something combative. But the good justice keeps on keeping on. And that only makes his fans love him more. This doesn't seem to happen to the other justices, by the way.

Each of the last few Supreme Court terms has seen Scalia test the bounds of judicial impartiality. In 2003, he went so far as to recuse himself from hearing what would have been one of the most important church-state cases of his career, the test of whether the words "under God" in the Pledge of Allegiance impermissibly impose religion into the lives of public-school students. Scalia didn't explain his recusal; the justices almost never do. But it's likely because of an earlier speech he gave in which he suggested the pledge case had been wrongly decided in the 9th Circuit.

In 2004, having gone duck hunting in Louisiana with Vice President Dick Cheney while Cheney was the named party in a case pending before the Supreme Court, the justice refused to step aside, flippantly telling the *Los Angeles Times* that "I do not think my impartiality could reasonably be questioned" and that the only thing really wrong with the trip was that the hunting was "lousy." The justice went on to file a lengthy 21-page "memorandum" explaining to the public why he would not recuse himself for this or other "silly" improprieties.

In 2006, with a case about the procedural rights of enemy combatants held at Guantanamo Bay pending before the court, Scalia gave a speech in Switzerland in which he said, among other things: "War is war, and it has never been the case that when you captured a combatant you have to give them a jury trial in your civil courts. . . . Give me a break." Of the rights of Guantanamo detainees captured on a battlefield he added, "If he was captured by my army on a battlefield, that is where he belongs. I had a son on that battlefield and they were shooting at my son and I'm not about to give this man who was captured in a war a full jury trial. I mean it's crazy."

It wasn't merely that Scalia was suggesting that he had already made up his mind on a matter the court would hear only weeks later. It wasn't merely the dismissive words he chose to characterize the opposing legal view: "that's crazy," or "give me a break." The problem was also that he was suggesting that his son's service in Iraq made him emotionally invested and thus less than impartial. When his recusal was sought in the case, Scalia did not comply. Only days later he was involved in a verbal flap with a Boston reporter that ended with a gesture that she characterized as obscene.

In a letter to her editor, Scalia called it "Sicilian."

Is this brilliant jurist losing his mind? Is he so frustrated by 17 years of failure to sway an allegedly conservative court to his side on social issues that he no longer cares who he offends or how biased he may appear? Has he become so swept up by the Coulter/Limbaugh/O'Reilly game of court-bashing that he cannot see how damaging it is when played by a justice? Or is he running for elected office? What possesses Justice Scalia to eschew the reclusive public life of many justices, or at least the blandly apolitical public lives of most, to play the role of benighted public intellectual and knight gallant in the culture wars?

The rule for improper judicial speech is set forth in Title 28, Section 455, of the U.S. Code, providing that judges must recuse themselves in any case in which their "impartiality might reasonably be questioned." With his comments in about the Pledge of Allegiance, Scalia showed that—at least on that case—he did not have an open mind. One of the reasons Scalia was so quick to recuse himself (and the decision was his alone to make) is that he is intellectually honest enough to know that he slipped up by discussing a case that would come before the court. The later comments he made about enemy combatants arguably just echoed a dissent he'd written in an earlier case in the War on Terror. As a technical matter, his recusal in the Pledge case was a necessity while his recusal in the Guantanamo case was not.

But the body of his speeches and addresses makes it clear that he appears anything but "impartial" as is seemingly required by the law. One can predict his vote on most cases with great confidence. This is true of most justices, although Scalia would see it as a virtue: evidence of the consistency and predictability of his system of constitutional thinking. Whether or not judges should be held to views expressed in extrajudicial speeches and whether or not they should be forced to recuse themselves for them are once again open questions. Expect more recusal motions in the future. But the fact remains that judges who give controversial speeches imploring listeners to espouse certain views and values undermine the appearance of judicial neutrality, and Scalia is no stranger to this fact.

In 1996, with two euthanasia cases pending in the high court, Scalia was criticized for giving a speech claiming that there was "no constitutional right to die." In another 1996 case he said that

"Devout Christians are destined to be regarded as fools in modern society. . . . We are fools for Christ's sake. . . . We must pray for courage to endure the scorn of the sophisticated world." And in a 2002 speech, he urged any Catholic judge who agrees with the pope on capital punishment to resign from the bench.

One explanation for Scalia's pedantic bent is his background as a law professor at the universities of Virginia and Chicago, Stanford, and Georgetown. He loves to teach. There is a didactic quality to Scalia's performance on the bench—a sense in which he uses oral argument merely to lecture and browbeat his brethren—that is hard to escape. It is Scalia's way to joke, to tease, to interrupt, and to dominate his way through oral argument. He can never resist scoring the rhetorical point, answering his own or his colleagues' questions if the oral advocate fails to do so. The papers of former justice Thurgood Marshall reveal that Scalia's relentless sarcasm annoyed even his ideological ally, former chief justice William H. Rehnquist. And Scalia has always saved the worst of his venom for attacks on the court's "moderates," former justice Sandra Day O'Connor and Anthony Kennedy, whose defections to the left on social issues such as abortion and affirmative action engender a sense of almost personal intellectual betrayal.

Nothing enrages Scalia more than intellectual inconsistency. A decision that doesn't fit into the existing constitutional framework is to his mind a capital offense—worse even than horse-thieving. There is a wonderful line in the film *Broadcast News* that invariably calls Scalia to mind. Holly Hunter's boss snarls, "It must be nice to always believe you know better, to always know you are the smartest person in the room." To which Hunter replies, "No, it's awful." Scalia comes across as similarly burdened, beaten down by the weight of his own inevitable rightness.

Another key to understanding Scalia's tendency to run off at the mouth when standing at the lectern lies in his fixed system of constitutional interpretation. Scalia is the court's staunchest proponent of "originalism"—the doctrine holding that the Constitution is a dead document, not to be infused with the faddish new preferences of each generation's judges. In an article in *First Things*, from May 2002, Scalia made clear that he can freely opine on his views of capital punishment without jeopardizing the impartiality of his votes in any future cases precisely *because* his own vote is derived strictly from the text of the Constitution, which is unwavering. In effect, said Scalia, his only job as a judge is to get out of the Framers' way as they rule the land. By casting himself, rather ghoulishly, as crypt-keeper rather than as judge, Scalia can render his personal morality and preferences immaterial. He can make all the speeches he wants without compromising his neutrality, simply by acting as the constitutional Ouija board he was meant to be.

But one cannot ignore—and Scalia would not have us ignore—the fact that he is also a deeply religious man. Scalia worships at a conservative Virginia church that erected a monument to unborn children several years back. And he joins many of the nation's religious groups in feeling besieged and marginalized by the constitutional wall that's been erected between church and state—a wall that keeps the devout from practicing and proselytizing in the public square. He is convinced that civilization is in decline and that this banishment of religion is directly responsible. He truly believes that the coarseness and callousness of modern mores and practices have imperiled us all. And if those beliefs make him sound more Jeremiah than Judge, well, Scalia would probably welcome the comparison.

This, then, is the insidious and brilliant part of the Antonin Scalia speaking tour: Merely by virtue of his public role, he is actually tearing down the wall between church and state every time he opens his mouth. Which is precisely what he wants.

Martha Stewart

She's a good thing.

BY DAVID PLOTZ

HERE IS A (PARTIAL) LIST OF OBJECTS that Martha Stewart has gilded: pomegranates, pumpkins, cookies, chocolate truffles, wrapping paper, oak leaves, acorns, and—no kidding—okra. The only thing Martha has not gilded is the lily. (But wait till it's back in season.)

Martha has proved that alchemy is not impossible: Brush enough gold paint on enough flora, and eventually you'll make real gold. Her stake in Martha Stewart Living Omnimedia—Omnimedia, has there ever been a more perfect name?—is worth around $1 billion. She has two TV shows, a Web site, a mail-order operation, several magazines, and dozens of books. Her stint in jail for lying about a stock trade has not dented her at all.

From the time she gutted her first cantaloupe through her time in prison, Martha has been an object of sniping and mockery. Traditionally, Martha has been battered by three criticisms. First, she is simply ludicrous. You could not imagine better comic material than her ideas of "living": the "midnight omelet dinner for 1,000"; the fruit baskets the size of a Chevy; the advice to make your own envelopes out of wood veneer, folding them with a bone knife. Parodies barely exaggerate when they imagine Martha turning water into wine ("a lovely Merlot") or manufacturing condoms from her own lamb. A second and more thoughtful batch of critics has charged her with encouraging class division, promoting soulless domestic conformism, and undermining working women by making them feel domestically inadequate.

The final criticism has been personal. Her trial exposed her icy, brutal behavior to underlings. An unauthorized biography, *Just Desserts*, contends that she abused her (now ex-) husband, ignores her daughter, belittles her mother, sues her gardener for pennies, plagiarizes recipes from better cooks, and humiliates her staff. Her fabled "Remembering" columns are a hash of bunkum and hyperbole. The persona she cultivates—the warm, welcoming hostess with a close-knit family—is a fraud.

These criticisms have subsided. Martha's prison stint allegedly cured her egomania (New! Improved! Now 75 percent more humble!) Her *Apprentice* charmed critics who expected Trumpishness (though viewers didn't like it so much). She is benefiting from parody fatigue as well. She has been a figure of fun since *Entertaining* was published in 1982, so all the jokes are old.

But the subsiding criticism also represents a long-overdue recognition that Martha is, as she would say, a Good Thing. In one TV interview, she described herself as a "teacher. . . . We are offering information, high-quality, well-researched, how-to information." What she does is not silly at all, or at least no more silly than most advice magazines. Her magazines and TV shows retain just enough nonsense to make them irksome ("sew your own pashmina from home-raised llamas," and the like), but she supplies valuable instruction about the mundane tasks of life. *Martha Stewart Living* helped pioneer the lifestyle utility magazine. The do-it-yourself ethos promoted by *Cook's Illustrated* and *Make* has been Martha's stock in trade for 20 years. It is not false consciousness that makes tens of millions of people follow Martha every month. It is her good advice.

But the great achievement of Martha's domestic gospel is not practical but moral. She has a puritanical sensibility. She believes in the uplifting power of work. She instructs you so that you will know how to create objects yourself, grow plants yourself, learn home repair yourself, cook food yourself. Doing something well is good and liberating and fulfilling. It strengthens friendships and families: When I saw her making waffles, it made me want to make waffles. If I make waffles, I will invite the downstairs neighbors up to eat them, and that is undoubtedly a Good Thing.

Martha practices materialism, but not consumerism. She believes, rightly, that it makes you wiser and happier to cook your own applesauce than to buy it. Well, you may say, it's easy for her to make homemade applesauce. That's her job. But she did it when it wasn't her job, too. Even if most viewers rarely practice anything Martha preaches—she calls such slackers "Martha Dreamers" as opposed to "Martha Doers"—she is still a worthy goad.

Her DIY credo makes Martha democratically snobbish. She hews to a country-house sensibility, but anyone can follow it. It doesn't cost much, because you do it yourself. If a middle-class Polish girl like Martha can blossom into an affected, Breck-girl faux-WASP, you can too!

There is a sexism in the criticism of Martha's fraudulent persona and monomaniacal perfectionism. The female domestic tycoon is obliged to behave better than the guys. (This is why Oprah's private life is examined more carefully than David Letterman's.)

Fortunately, commerce has finally trumped personality. As *The Apprentice* demonstrated, Martha is now known most as the CEO of a company called Omnimedia, not as a bitchy hausfrau. We admire perfectionist monomania in Google tycoons, so why not in Martha? Politicians get away with advertising bogus family bliss; Martha should too. Martha shows us how to make a romantic dinner for the husband she doesn't have, host a party for the kids she doesn't like, bake muffins for the neighbors who hate her. But those are her tragedies, not our business (or Wall Street's). The muffins are still tasty, and that's what matters.

Bruce Springsteen

Why I still love him.

BY STEPHEN METCALF

IN HIS EARLY LIVE SHOWS, Bruce Springsteen had a habit of rattling off, while the band vamped softly in the background, some thoroughly implausible story from his youth. This he punctuated with a shy, wheezing laugh that let you know he didn't for a second buy into his own bullshit. Back then, in the early 1970s, Bruce was still a regional act, touring the dive bars and dive colleges of the Atlantic coast, playing any venue that would have him. As a matter of routine, a Springsteen show would kick off with audience members throwing gifts onto the stage. Not bras and panties, mind you, but gifts—something thoughtful, not too expensive. Bruce was one of their own, after all, a scrawny little dirtbag from the shore, a minor celebrity of what the great George Trow once called "the disappearing middle distance." By 1978, and the release of *Darkness on the Edge of Town*, the endearing Jersey wharf rat in Springsteen had been refined away. In its place was a majestic American simpleton with a generic heartland twang, obsessed with cars, Mary, the Man, and the bitterness between fathers and sons. Springsteen has been augmenting and refining that persona for so long now that it's hard to recall its status, not only as an invention, but an invention whose origin wasn't even Bruce Springsteen. For all the po-faced mythic resonance that now accompanies Bruce's every move, we can thank Jon Landau, the ex–*Rolling Stone* critic who, after catching a typically seismic

Springsteen set in 1974, famously wrote, "I saw rock and roll's future, and its name is Bruce Springsteen."

Well, Bruce Springsteen was Jon Landau's future. Over the next couple of years, Landau insinuated himself into Bruce's artistic life and consciousness (while remaining on the *Rolling Stone* masthead) until he became Springsteen's producer, manager, and full-service Svengali. Unlike the down-on-their-luck Springsteens of Freehold, N.J., Landau hailed from the well-appointed suburbs of Boston and had earned an honors degree in history from Brandeis. He filled his new protégé's head with an American Studies syllabus heavy on John Ford, Steinbeck, and Flannery O'Connor. At the same time that he intellectualized Bruce, he anti-intellectualized him. Rock music was transcendent, Landau believed, because it was primitive, not because it could be avant-garde. *The White Album* and Hendrix and the Velvet Underground had robbed rock of its power, which lay buried in the pre-Beatles era with Del Shannon and the Ronettes. Bruce's musical vocabulary accordingly shrank. By *Darkness on the Edge of Town*, gone were the West Side Story–esque jazz suites of *The Wild, the Innocent,* and the *E Street Shuffle*. In their place were tight, guitar-driven intro-verse-chorus-verse-bridge-chorus songs. Springsteen's image similarly transformed. On the cover of *Darkness*, he looks strangely like the sallower cousin of Pacino's Sonny Wortzik, the already quite sallow anti-hero of *Dog Day Afternoon*. The message was clear: Springsteen himself was one of the unbeautiful losers, flitting along the ghostly fringes of suburban respectability.

Thirty years later, and largely thanks to Landau, Springsteen is no longer a musician. He's a belief system. And, like any belief system worth its salt, he brooks no in-between. You're either in or you're out. This has solidified Bruce's standing with his base, for whom he remains a god of total rock authenticity. But it's killed him with everyone else. To a legion of devout nonbelievers—they're not saying Bruuuce, they're booing—Bruce is more a phenomenon akin to Dianetics or Tinkerbell than "the new Dylan," as the Columbia Records promotions machine once hyped him. And so we've reached a strange juncture. About America's last rock star, it's either Pentecostal enthusiasm or total disdain.

To walk back from this impasse, we need to see Springsteen's persona for what it really is: Jon Landau's middle-class fantasy of white, working-class authenticity. Does it derogate Springsteen to claim that he is, in essence, a white minstrel act? Not at all. Only by peeling back all the layers of awful heartland authenticity and rediscovering the old Jersey bullshitter underneath can we begin to grasp the actual charms of the man and his music. A glimpse of this old bullshitter was on display when Springsteen inducted U2 into the Rock 'n' Roll Hall of Fame in 2005. Springsteen had recently seen an iPod commercial featuring the Irish rockers. "Now personally, I live an insanely expensive lifestyle that my wife barely tolerates," the old BSer confided to the audience of industry heavyweights, adding,

> Now, I burn money, and that calls for huge amounts of cash flow. But, I also have a ludicrous image of myself that keeps me from truly cashing in. You can see my problem. Woe is me. So the next morning, I call up Jon Landau . . . and I say, "Did you see that iPod thing?" and he says, "Yes." And he says, "And I hear they didn't take any money." And I said, "They didn't take any money?" and he says, "No." I said, "Smart, wily Irish guys. Anybody—anybody—can do an ad and take the money. But to do the ad and not take the money . . . that's smart. That's wily." I say, "Jon, I want you to call up Bill Gates or whoever is behind this thing and float this: a red, white and blue iPod signed by Bruce 'The Boss' Springsteen. Now remember, no matter how much money he offers, don't take it!"

Every now and again, the majestic simpleton breaks character and winks; and about as often, he works his way back to subtlety and a human scale and cuts a pretty great song or album. From the post-Landau period, the harrowing masterpiece *Nebraska* is the only record you can push on the nonbelievers, followed by the grossly underrated *Tunnel of Love*. The Oscar-winning "Streets of Philadelphia," an account of a man with AIDS slowly fading into his own living ghost, is the equal of any song he's written. In 1995 Springsteen produced *The Ghost of Tom Joad*, the culmination of a 15-year obsession with Woody Guthrie, whose biography he had been handed the night after Reagan defeated Carter, in 1980. The album is stronger than its popular reception might lead one to believe. "Across the Border" and "Galveston Bay" are lovely and understated and bring home the fact that Springsteen—a man who wrote monster hits for acts as diverse as Manfred Mann, the Pointer Sisters, and Patti Smith—remains a skilled melodist. Nonetheless, the record is a little distant in its sympathies, as if Springsteen had thumbed through back issues of *The Utne Reader* before sitting down to compose.

His 2005 album *Devils & Dust* is a sequel to *The Ghost of Tom Joad*. It's mostly acoustic and intimate in scale; but Springsteen appears to have taken criticism of *Tom Joad* to heart, and *Devils & Dust* is warmer, and in patches, fully up-tempo. It's hard to describe how good the good songs are. The title song is classic Springsteen—"a dirty wind's blowing," and a young soldier may "kill the things he loves" to survive. And on "Black Cowboys," Springsteen unites a visionary concision of detail with long lines in a way that channels William Blake:

> Come the fall the rain flooded these homes, here in Ezekiel's valley of dry bones, it fell hard and dark to the ground. It fell without a sound. Lynette took up with a man whose business was the boulevard, whose smile was fixed in a face that was never off guard.

Though initially signed as a folkie, Springsteen has never been much of a technician on the acoustic guitar, compared to, say, the infinitely nimble Richard Thompson. But on *Devils & Dust* there's a new comfort with the instrument. Ah, but how hard the lapses in taste! The strings and vocal choruses used to punch up the sound are—what other word is there?—corny. *Devils & Dust* too often sounds like a chain store selling faux Americana bric-a-brac. One always suspects with Springsteen that, in addition to a blonde Telecaster and "the Big Man," a focus group lies close at hand. The album is suspiciously tuned in to two recent trends, the exploding population of the Arizona and New Mexico exurbs; and the growing religiosity of the country as a whole. *Devils & Dust* is very *South by Southwest*—Mary is now Maria, there's a lot of mesquite and scrub pine, and one song even comes with a handy key to its regional terminology (Mustaneros: Mustangers; Pradera: Prairie; Riata: Rope). It's also crammed with biblical imagery, from a modern retelling of the story of Leah to Christ's final solacing of his mother. The first is a silly throwaway; the second is a fetching, Dylan-inspired hymn that ends with the teasing rumination, "Well Jesus kissed his mother's hands/ Whispered, 'Mother, still your tears,/ For remember the soul of the universe/ Willed a world and it appeared.' "

The high watermark for Springsteen commercially, of course, was 1984, when *Born in the USA* somehow caught both the feelings of social dislocation and the euphoric jingoism of the Reagan era. Landau's mythic creation, the blue-collar, rock 'n' roll naïf, has never held such broad appeal since. In recent years, Springsteen has settled into a pattern of selling a couple million albums (*Born in the USA* sold 15 million) to the Bruce die-hards. A clue to who these people are can be found in Springsteen's evolving persona, which is no longer as structured around his own working-class roots. Springsteen has said he tries to "disappear" into the voices of the migrant workers and ghetto prisoners whose stories make up *Devils & Dust*: "What would they do, what wouldn't they do, how would they behave in this circumstance, the rhythm of their speech, that's sort of where the music comes in." With Landau nowhere in evidence (he's thanked, but excluded from the album's formal credits), it is up to Springsteen alone to impersonate the voices of the dispossessed. The pupil has finally surpassed the master.

Nonetheless, here I am, starting to hum its tunes, growing a little devil's patch, hitting the gym, and adding a distant heartland twang to my speech. (My wife, meanwhile, curls up on the sofa in shame.) You old bullshitter, you got me again.

Rachael Ray

Food snobs should quit picking on her.

BY JILL HUNTER PELLETTIERI

RACHAEL RAY MAY BE the world's most reviled chef. Entire blogs are devoted to slamming the perky Food Network superstar—"Rachael Ray Sucks" is particularly vicious. On Web sites like eGullet, a "society for culinary arts and letters," users say she should be "tarred and feathered." And professional chefs turn up their noses when Ray comes around. It's easy to see why: Ray rejects specialty ingredients, elaborate recipes, and other foodie staples. But she deserves our respect. She understands how Americans really cook, and she's an exceptional entertainer.

Ray's marquee program, *30-Minute Meals*, relies on countless foodie no-nos. She advocates store-bought shortcuts—"I take a little help where I can get it"—using boxed corn muffin mix for her Cracked Corn and Cheese Squares, and chunky peanut butter in her Thai Salad With Peanut Dressing. She loathes baking—it's too fussy—so her "homemade" desserts are things like Black Cherry Ice Cream With Chocolate Sauce: Buy the ice cream and top with chocolate sauce and a dash of cherry liqueur (Reddi-Wip is optional). Her dishes rely solely on items available at the local Safeway. And she's no stranger to fast food: She endorsed a Burger King chicken sandwich in 2003.

Ray's ditzy demeanor also makes her easy to dismiss. She giggles off-cue and constantly praises her own cooking. "Smells awesome already!" she says, making her Snapper in a Snap. "I am so psyched about that." She employs kitschy abbreviations—EVOO means "extra virgin olive oil"—and gives her menus corny nicknames like You-Won't-Be-Single-for-Long Vodka Cream Pasta. The acknowledgments in her *$40 a Day* cookbook read like a high-school yearbook: "Don . . . You are the tallest man we've ever had on crew, and yet you pack the smallest bag—ever! Cool." And it didn't boost her credibility when she posed for pinup shots in *FHM*. (One featured Ray licking chocolate off a spoon.) When the magazine hit newsstands, she said, "I think it is kinda cool for someone who is goofy, and a cook, just a normal person to be thought of in that way."

Today Ray is hardly "normal"—she's a multimedia queen. Since Ray joined the Food Network in 2001, she's slowly taken over. In addition to *30-Minute Meals*, she gossips with celebrities on *Inside Dish and* hosts two travel shows, *$40 a Day* and her latest program, *Tasty Travels*. Her cookbooks are perpetual inhabitants of the best-seller list. When she touted Wüsthof's Santoku knife, sales spiked; she now endorses her own blade. She even has her own magazine: *Every Day with Rachael Ray*. Just like Oprah and Martha!

To her credit, Ray has always cast herself as a sort of anti-Martha, offering options for those who want to save money, eat healthfully, and cook at home but don't have the time or budget to entertain the Turkey Hill way. Too busy to hunt down authentic ingredients at ethnic markets? Make Chicken Curry in a Hurry instead. She also offers quick versions of slow-cooked classics like stew or chicken and dumplings, so working parents can still serve comfort foods on cold winter nights.

Ray's *30-Minute* shtick is simple, but inspired. Regular cooking shows are rife with annoying you'll-never-be-able-to-replicate-this moments. When the chef begins, meticulously prepared ingredients lie at the ready; he breezes through instruction and then—

poof!—pulls out the perfect frittata that's been waiting in the oven. Ray cooks in real time, so you know what you're in for.

The show is also fantastically entertaining. It's suspenseful: As the minutes tick by, Ray becomes frenetic—will she finish? (She always does.) And it's educational: As Ray trims her asparagus and frantically wraps prosciutto around the green stems, she offers tips. Use a "garbage bowl" to collect debris as you're cooking. Chop chicken into small pieces so it cooks faster. Roll citrus before you cut it, and you'll extract more juice. Forget about measuring—"Eyeball it!"

For years, I devoured the show, and Ray and I enjoyed a problem-free relationship. But as she became more popular and her detractors became more vocal, I realized that if I wanted to defend her, I should try a few of her recipes. You can imagine my dismay when, 21 recipes later, I was forced to admit that I could not complete a 30-Minute Meal in 30 minutes. Ray's four-course "Cooking for 10 in 30 Italian Style" menu took me a frenzied one hour, 25 minutes, and 57 seconds. Though the food was very good, I came away exhausted and with a burnt finger. My most successful effort was Ray's "Back in the Day" menu: Super Sloppy Joes, Deviled Potato Salad, and Root Beer Floats. I prepped with the same care as Ray—produce prerinsed, garbage bowl at the ready, pantry items near at hand—but it took me 49 minutes and 51 seconds (and I skipped the Root Beer Floats).

Where had I gone wrong? For a while, I suspected Ray of cutting corners. Was an army of interns frying chicken during commercials? But then I learned that Ray didn't start out on TV. Her first "30-Minute Meals" were devised for a series of cooking classes that she taught at Cowan & Lobel, a gourmet grocery store in Albany, N.Y. (The classes eventually earned her a regular spot on the local news.) Back then, Ray prepared her meals for a live audience, which means she couldn't cheat: She had to rely on smart kitchen choreography. Ray may have a crack production team at her disposal today, but she still exhibits considerable logistical acumen.

Unlike most celebrated chefs, Ray seems to have spent more time in supermarkets than cooking in restaurant kitchens. She started out working the candy counter at Macy's Marketplace in New York and then managed the fresh foods department there; later she became a manager and buyer for Manhattan grocer Agata & Valentina. That's probably why she's so good at adapting gastronomy for the masses: She knows how real people shop and eat.

Her Super Sloppy Joes certainly aren't haute cuisine, but that's no reason for highfalutin chefs to knock her. Consider what Ray brings to the table: creativity, adeptness, speed. Her skills are as estimable as those of any Michelin-star-winning chef, and they're far more practical. I may have abandoned my Rachael Ray time trials, but I'm still making "30-Minute Meals." And you know what? They do smell awesome.

Thomas Friedman

What makes the *Times*man a great columnist?

BY DAVID PLOTZ

SAUDI PRINCES TEST PEACE PROPOSALS in Tom Friedman's column. His latest book, *The Earth Is Flat*, is a monster best-seller (in part because every aspiring president, CEO, and Davos attendee has bought 10 copies). And he's even been suggested as a presidential candidate (though for whom? The Flat Earth Party?). All this means it's tempting to start comparing him to Walter Lippmann or Joe Alsop. After all, there is something very old school about the kind of fame and hobnobbing with foreign policy grandees that Friedman now traffics in. In fact, Friedman does not resemble the old-timers in any meaningful way. He has become the most important journalist in the post–9/11 world for three rather modern reasons.

The first is that his economic theories give him both intellectual credibility and—more significantly—an optimistic framework for understanding geopolitics. The jolly globalism in Friedman's books is not profound—more serious economists grumble about his cheery oversimplifications and catchphrases. But it provides him with a positive way to examine world problems that both gloomy conservatives and anticapitalists lefties lack. In Friedman's worldview, solutions to the most intractable world problems are around the corner: The market can help us all, once we can persuade people to shelve their hatreds and act rationally for a few minutes. Like David Brooks, who shares his penchant for sanguineness and grand theorizing, Friedman is much more enjoyable to read than most of the negativoids in OpEdistan. You know he will always look for a solution.

This is not to say Friedman is a rosy-glassed idealist—which brings us to the second reason for his recent success. Friedman has emerged as the best explainer of how the United States should relate to the Arab, Muslim, and Israeli worlds. This is not because of ideology, or rhetorical brilliance, or even analytical power, but because of his gritty, intimate knowledge of the places he is writing about.

Before September 11, Friedman's twice-weekly column was steady but not spectacular. He proselytized about globalism, criticized missile defense, and had many kind words for the European Union. He was a maybe-read, not a must.

But Friedman, who's in his early 50s, spent five years in Beirut for the *New York Times* and five more in Jerusalem (winning a Pulitzer in each city). For most of his journalistic career, Friedman thought about nothing but Arabs, Muslims, and Israelis. 9/11 reunited him with his one true love.

Friedman, who has always reported more than most columnists, has been a beaver since September 11. In the six months after the attacks, he made six overseas trips to 13 countries, including every important nation in the Middle East and Central Asia. He probably traveled more in the region and talked to more relevant people than any American official—which may explain why he seemed to understand the political opportunities and obstacles so much better than our politicians did. Friedman builds his columns on the details of this reporting. "I'm not smart enough to smoke a pipe, put on a cardigan, and throw down thunderbolts," he says. Many reporters have all the facts, and many columnists have a pugnacious and bossy temperament: Friedman is the rare journalist who has both.

Friedman's principal task for the past five years has been explaining the failures of the Islamic world. Why did Saudi Arabia spawn Osama Bin Laden and 15 of the 19 hijackers? Why is anti-Americanism so rampant in the Middle East? Why do so many Arabs and Muslims sympathize with violent Islamists? And what can we do about all this? Friedman, drawing on his reporting trips, has argued that the anti-democratic, authoritarian Arab regimes—notably our "friends" Egypt and Saudi Arabia—have encouraged anti-Americanism and anti-Semitism to prevent popular dissent. The Arab world obsesses over its grievances and relies on oil wealth rather than developing decent educational systems and building strong economies. Angry young men embrace radical Islam rather than heed their corrupt, bankrupt governments. The United States, Friedman insists, must stop coddling our friendly Arab dictators and demand openness, rule of law, better education, and more democracy. Globalization can drag these nations into the Lexus world, but only if their citizens reject the atavistic hatred and grudges that now shackle them. In the meantime, the U.S. needs an energy crusade to wean us from foreign oil, saving billions that we are spending to prop up grotesque governments.

Friedman's columns, which are widely distributed worldwide, have enraged many in the Middle East. He has demonstrated an admirable knack for making friends of his enemies and enemies of his friends. He has long been tolerated in the Arab world because he condemns Israeli settlement building and because he exposed Israel's culpability in the Sabra and Shatilla massacres. For the same reasons, the Israeli and American Jewish right-wing detested him as a traitor, calling him "anti-Zionist." Some right-wing Jewish leaders have suggested he shouldn't be invited to speak to Jewish audiences, because he's an enemy of the Jewish people. But these days, Friedman's criticism of Arab regimes and the Palestinians has endeared him to Israelis and American Jews and cost him in the Arab world.

The third reason for Friedman's success is that he's an unabashed populist, unlike the Olympian columnists of yore. They made their columns from what they learned in private conversations. But this is an age when opinion journalism has abandoned the backrooms of power for the green rooms of Fox News Channel. Friedman is a star because he's incredibly comfortable with the give-and-take of TV punditry and unapologetic about wanting to use TV to reach the broad audience.

Friedman, it must be said, is not much of a stylist. He endlessly repeats favorite themes: How many "open letters from blah to blah" can one columnist write? No philosophical foundation girds his work. He doesn't quote Spengler or Gibbon. Friedman, a Minnesotan, is a proud small-d democrat (and probably large-D Democrat, too). He epitomizes the middle-browing of the *Times*. But this does not mean his writing lacks power. Friedman's skill is that he speaks in the voice of Madison Avenue. He's effective not because he sounds like a historian, but because he sounds like an advertisement. Friedman has no ideas that can't be expressed in a catchphrase. His work is salted with slogans and phrases in capital letters. They are gimmicky, too simple, and extremely useful. Some don't stick: What is "Globalution," a favorite term from his book *The Lexus and the Olive Tree*? But many do, and they are why Friedman lasts. "The Earth Is Flat" has practically supplanted the term globalism (in part because Friedman uses the phrase in so many of his columns. He changed the way many Americans think about Arab governments with the phrase "Hama Rules," his description of how Arab leaders ruthlessly extinguish dissent. "The Golden Arches Theory of Conflict Prevention," which argued that countries with McDonald's restaurants (that is, middle-class countries) don't go to war against each other, is incredibly popular. "Fast World" and "Slow World," other terms for understanding globalism, are memorable.

Friedman's post–9/11 refrains are enduring, too. "Yes, but," his term for Arab ambivalence about the 9/11 attacks, was quoted back to me repeatedly by admirers. Friedman lectured the Saudis that they need to train and educate their own citizens by drilling "human oil wells."

One of Friedman's most appealing qualities is his essential pragmatism. Friedman is sometimes linked with Robert Kaplan, the other famous pop analyst of the Middle East and globalization. Kaplan is pessimistic and hopeless, believing that religious divisions, ethnic rage, and ancient hatreds inevitably doom most of the world to chaos. Kaplan's idea of foreign policy sometimes seems to be a shrug and an M-16.

But Friedman has not an ideological bone in his body. He is willing to try anything. Some critics think that makes him a weathervane. But there is a more charitable view. In a region of persistent hatreds, a certain flexibility is necessary. Consider Friedman's views on the Israeli-Palestinian peace process. Friedman was a staunch supporter of the 2000 Camp David accords. They didn't happen. When the Palestinians launched their recent, suicidal intifada, Friedman floated the idea that Israel hand over the occupied territories to NATO. That didn't go anywhere. Then he floated Saudi Crown Prince Abdullah's proposal that Israel pull back to its 1967 borders in exchange for full Arab recognition. Also dead in the water. And then another plan. And then another. Friedman refuses to give up. If at first you don't succeed, then write, write again.

U2

Their vague majesties of rock.

BY DAVID PLOTZ

IT HAS BEEN AN ASTONISHING 21st century for U2. After its disastrous '90s flirtation with irony, the Irish quartet returned to the swaddling comfort of earnestness at just the right moment. U2's 2000 album *All That You Can't Leave Behind*—a throwback to the sweeping righteous love of *The Joshua Tree* and *The Unforgettable Fire*—drew raves from critics and hit number 1 in more than 30 countries. Its 2004 follow-up, *How to Dismantle an Atomic Bomb,* received even better reviews, went to number 1 in 34 countries, and has sold more than 9 million copies. The band has headlined a Super Bowl halftime show, won several armfuls of Grammies, and run two of the most successful concert tours in world history. In 2005, U2 was inducted into the Rock and Roll Hall of Fame—the rare case of that honor arriving before a band started embarrassing itself. U2's iPod endorsement performed an unheard-of twofer: It made both the band and the product seem cooler. Since September 11, their super-sincerity has been in particularly high demand. Both "Walk On" and the old hit "One" became September 11 anthems. Meanwhile, Bono's debt-relief campaign has won him praise all over the world, as well as *Time*'s 2005 "Man of the Year" title (shared with Bill and Melinda Gates).

U2 has now been good longer than any other important band in history. The Rolling Stones have been around forever, but their creative period lasted only 15 years. The Beatles imploded after a decade. U2—the same lineup of Bono, the Edge, Adam Clayton, and Larry Mullen—has been making acclaimed albums since 1980's *Boy*.

The band's achievements depend on two neat tricks. First, Bono—the public face of U2—has a genius for cognitive dissonance. He is the upstairs, downstairs king of rock: He simultaneously inflates himself into the most grandiose, arrogant, self-righteous rock star and deflates himself with self-mockery and modesty. He describes U2 as reapplying for the position of "best band in the world"; calls the band "magic" and "extraordinary"; announces on *Rattle & Hum* that "All I have is a red guitar, three chords, and the truth"; and insists that "We've always been about more than music. We're about spirituality. We're about the world we live in."

But Bono counters every claim of godliness by throwing a pie in his own face. Asked by an interviewer if he is a pioneer, he declares that he is "one of the inventors of the mullet." The band mocked themselves on *The Simpsons*. Bono cheerfully disses his own political activism: "The only thing worse than a rock star is a rock star with a conscience."

Both stances are sincere, and it is a very winning combination. The worshipful fans adore the earnest grandiosity and sing along as Bono claims transcendence. A U2 concert is one of the few places on the planet where intelligent people wave cigarette lighters without irony. In those moments when you want to believe that rock music is something bigger than entertainment—and who doesn't haven't such moments?—U2 offers exalted nourishment. They're about more than music, man. They're about spirituality. They are the unforgettable fire!

But U2's self-consciousness inoculates them against critics, who can find no point of attack. If you ridicule Bono for his pomposity, he will not only laugh at the joke, but will twist the knife deeper in his own chest. They are grand spectacle, but with a wink for those who are looking for one. The combination of self-important grandeur and self-deprecating humor is exceptionally rare, especially among celebrities. Many popular musicians have one or the other (almost always the self-important grandeur). The few that have both—the Rolling Stones, the Beatles, and Elton John are at the top of the short list—can survive greatness and don't get destroyed by their pretensions (as did humorless sorts such as the Doors, Guns N' Roses, Led Zeppelin . . .).

U2's other trick is to pretend that it is a political rock band. It's true that U2 is politically promiscuous. The liner notes for *All That You Can't Leave Behind*, for example, endorse Amnesty International, Greenpeace, the charity War Child, the Jubilee 2000 debt-relief campaign, freedom for Burma, and justice in Sierra Leone. And that's just one album. U2's roster of cause songs includes: "Sunday Bloody Sunday" (one of many about Ireland's troubles); "Seconds" (nuclear war); "The Unforgettable Fire" (also nuclear war); "Pride (In the Name of Love)" (Martin Luther King Jr.); "MLK" (also Martin Luther King Jr.); "Bullet the Blue Sky" (U.S. Central America policy); and so on.

It's also true that Bono is exceptionally political offstage. His admirable debt campaign has brought celebrity wattage to an extremely unhip issue, as Bono has proved an exceptional Washington lobbyist, a supremely good schmoozer, and a genius at explaining a complicated issue with clarity and sincerity. It is no exaggeration to say that Bono has done more than any pope or financier or president to cancel the debts of basket-case third-world countries. But U2 has duped their fans into believing their *music* is political too. Bono declares that his songs are about this or that cause, but no fan could ever know that from listening. "Walk On" is supposedly about Burmese democracy activist Aung San Suu Kyi. Will someone please listen to it and tell me what it has to do with Burma? I adore "Pride (In the Name of Love)" as much as anyone, but I defy you to explain what it teaches about Martin Luther King Jr.

U2 is perhaps the world's vaguest band. If a U2 song isn't written in the first person, it is penned to an unnamed, indistinct "you." Instead of stories or wordplay, they rely solely on fuzzy imagery. I opened the liner notes to *All That You* . . . and wrote down the first three lines I read: "See the canyons broken by clouds"; "I and I in the sky"; "A man takes a rocket ship into the skies." Classic U2 haze—skies, rockets, clouds, canyons. Doesn't anyone have a name? There are never any actual people in U2 songs, never any characters. (Compare U2 to the narrative specificity of Bob Dylan or Bruce Springsteen.) This vagueness drains U2's lyrics of any content: It is impossible to think about a U2 song. "One" includes depressing lines like "We hurt each other/ Then we do it again" and "You say love is a temple. . . . You ask me to enter/ But then you make me crawl"—yet this hasn't stopped fans from turning it into a September 11 anthem. If it is political music, it is for the Bob Kerreys of the world, for folks who seem full of great, but totally inchoate, ideas.

U2's music—especially the Edge's soaring guitars—supports this lyrical vagueness. Their songs are gorgeous and majestic, but they produce only a single (though wonderful) emotion: a kind of lovely swelling of the soul.

This is the U2 paradox. Bono and Co. are constantly dedicating songs to specific causes, exhorting their fans to think and act in the world. Yet their music does exactly the opposite of what it intends. Politics is the process of channeling the heart into thought and action. U2's music declares that the heart is all that matters.

Dave Barry

Elegy for the humorist.

BY BRYAN CURTIS

DAVE BARRY, WHO QUIT HIS syndicated humor column in January 2005, was playing dumb for 22 years. Whenever someone suggested that Barry was our noblest social commentator, that he regularly makes the professionals of the *New York Times* editorial page look like bozos, Barry would point out that this was impossible, because, unlike most *Times*men, he took great pride in making booger jokes. Let us ignore that objection and repeat the suggestion. Dave Barry is—was—the most heroic newspaper columnist in America. He hides his considerable candlepower behind a jokester's guise of "Don't trust me, I'm just the comedian!" Or, as Barry himself once put it, "Readers are sometimes critical of me because just about everything I write about is an irresponsible lie."

Barry began his writing career in humiliating fashion. Slumming for a company called Burger Associates, he flew around the country teaching businessmen how to write interoffice memos. He also produced a syndicated humor column that ran in a few tiny newspapers and that practically nobody read. Barry came to the attention of Gene Weingarten, the editor of the *Miami Herald*'s Sunday magazine, *Tropic*, after freelancing an article on natural childbirth for a Philadelphia newspaper. "I read it and realized it was the first time in my life I had laughed out loud while reading the printed word," says Weingarten, who writes a humor column for the *Washington Post*. Barry began freelancing a monthly column for *Tropic*, which became biweekly, then weekly—and eventually landed Barry a full-time job at the *Herald*, where he holed up for the next two decades. Weingarten and his heirs deployed Barry as humorist, reporter, and quixotic political correspondent, such as the occasion when he began an interview with then-Gov. Bob Graham with a question about harmonica safety.

Weingarten suggests, tantalizingly, that Barry is something of a great brain—a suprising thing to say about a man who enjoys covering exploding livestock. "Dave had astonishingly high SAT scores," says Weingarten. "His humor is informed by an astounding intellect." One week, when *Tropic* converted itself into a kind of Devil's Dictionary, Weingarten instructed Barry to come up with a definition for "sense of humor." Barry disappeared from the office for a few days. He came back with this: "A sense of humor is a measurement of the extent to which we realize that we are trapped in a world almost totally devoid of reason. Laughter is how we express the anxiety we feel at this knowledge." Then he promptly went back to writing about exploding livestock.

Barry evades questions about what makes his writing funny. (In a column, he once suggested it was his copious use of the word "weasel.") Weingarten says Barry codified one rule of comedy: "Put the funniest word at the end of sentence." A second Barry rule of comedy might be: "Put the funniest sentence at the beginning of the story." Barry writes some of the jazziest opening lines in the business. This is partly out of necessity, since Barry's column usually runs about 800 words. It can take up to a minute or two to unwrap a humor piece by the *New Yorker*'s Ian Frazier or Steve Martin, compared to mere seconds for one by Barry. Among Barry's best openers:

"Without my eyeglasses, I have a great deal of trouble distinguishing between house fires and beer signs."

"I have received a disturbing letter from Mr. Frank J. Phillips, who describes himself as both a patriot and a Latin teacher."

"Like most Americans, I was thrilled to death last February when our wealthy yachting snots won the coveted America's Cup back from Australia's wealthy yachting snots."

"At the *Miami Herald* we ordinarily don't provide extensive coverage of New York City unless a major news development occurs up there, such as Sean Penn coming out of a restaurant."

Next, we move to Barry's third rule of comedy, which is to change subjects as frequently and jarringly as possible, often beginning with the second sentence of the article. Last July, for example, Barry began a column wondering why breakfast-cereal mascots—Toucan Sam, Cap'n Crunch, et al.—were uniformly male. A few hundred words later, Barry had forgotten about that idea and was asking whether we should ditch the phrase "the birds and the bees" for a more zoologically-correct expression, "the dogs."

Because he's read by boomers and teenagers alike, Barry is often thought of as a guileless, domestic funnyman. (In *Dave's World*, a sitcom based on his life, he was played by the irritatingly sweet Harry Anderson.) And, true, Barry wrote plenty of sweet columns about his son, his dogs (Earnest and Zippy, themselves comic icons), and his lifelong battle with recalcitrant air conditioners. But Barry wrote an astonishing amount about politics, too. Few know, perhaps, that his book *Dave Barry's Greatest Hits* contains two columns about airline deregulation. And another about tax reform. And another about the defense of Western Europe. And that in his book about American history, *Dave Barry Slept Here*, he inveighed, comically, against the Hawley-Smoot Tariff ("the most terrible and destructive event in the history of Mankind"). And that from the Democratic Convention—he's covered a half-dozen—he wrote (correctly) that poor John Glenn "couldn't electrify a fish tank if he threw a toaster in it."

In 1987, after the *New York Times* published one of its bleak articles about South Florida ("Can Miami Save Itself?"), Barry's editors dispatched their man to New York to give the *Times* its comeuppance. Barry returned with a wicked 4,000-word story in which he gently pointed out that Ed Koch's Manhattan was a food court of urban decay and drug paraphernalia, too. Where the *Times'* story had been heavy-handed and sober, Barry was impish, reporting, "[W]e immediately detect signs of a healthy economy in the form of people squatting on the sidewalk selling realistic jewelry." The denizens of Times Square, he observed, were "very friendly, often coming right up and offering to engage in acts of leisure with you." After catching a cab at LaGuardia Airport, Barry formulated the three immutable laws of New York taxis:

1. DRIVER SPEAKS NO ENGLISH.
2. DRIVER JUST GOT HERE TWO DAYS AGO FROM SOMEPLACE LIKE SENEGAL.
3. DRIVER HATES YOU.

Barry (not the *Times*) won the Pulitzer Prize for commentary the next year. And perhaps his gifts as a political satirist point toward a second act. In his valedictory column, Barry refused to rule out a return to column-writing, and he has lately kept himself sharp on his blog. Here's an idea: As soon as the next *Times*man shuffles off to the Old Columnists' Home, put Barry smack dab in the middle of the *Times* editorial page. Barry confessed a few years ago that he's a raving libertarian—just the kind of dyspeptic crank who would take pleasure in thumbing Washington in the eye. Give him 14 inches twice a week and let him write whatever he wants. Why settle for another depressingly sober columnist when you can have one who makes booger jokes?

Bob Dylan

Why he's still with us.

BY DAVID PLOTZ

IN RECENT PHOTOS OF BOB DYLAN, he's wearing a lopsided, bemused grin, the smile of someone who can't quite believe what's happening to him. If you were Dylan, you'd be puzzled, too. The past few years have been one long victory lap for Dylan. His 2004 memoir, *Chronicles, Volume I,* was lavished with praise. Martin Scorcese released a hagiographic documentary, *No Direction Home*, a year later. The president and Washington's elite paid homage to the singer at the Kennedy Center Honors—an event that usually celebrates ancient respectables in the Bob Hope/Tony Bennett vein. Dylan shaved and even wore a tuxedo. Having all but shut Dylan out of the Grammies for the first 35 years of his career, the recording industry lavished three awards on his 1997 album *Time Out of Mind*, including Album of the Year, and another one on his 2001 release *Love and Theft*. Oh, and he appeared in a Victoria's Secret ad.

There is general agreement that the Dylan honors signify Something Very Important about the '60s. The most popular explanation is a political one: Dylan in a tux is the final, ironic nail in the counterculture coffin. The establishment has finally co-opted the ultimate anti-establishment figure. Dylan, the story goes, was the icon for the lefty politics of the '60s: He sang "Blowin' in the Wind" and "Masters of War" and was the role model for a generation of protestors. Once he sang, "Don't follow leaders." Now—sniff—he's hanging out with the president.

But this is a misapprehension of Dylan. He was never as much of a counterculturist as his fans believed, and he was certainly never much of a politico. Except for a brief, awkward foray into the civil rights movement, Dylan essentially ignored political activism during the '60s. At a time when every musician spoke out against the Vietnam War, Dylan did not. He ignored presidential campaigns and lefty crusades. In *Chronicles,* he writes that he explicitly tried to avoid being the voice of his generation. He never preached, or much sympathized with, hippie rhetoric. He denied, and still denies, that his songs had a political significance: He licensed "The Times They Are A-Changin'" for a bank advertisement.

If there is a decade of which Dylan is a symbol, it's the '70s. He has always pursued self-actualization rather than protest, artistic fulfillment rather than politics. Pause for requisite Dylan mantra: "He not busy being born is busy dying." (For a personal-growth slogan, this is pretty gloomy. But it is a pretty grim song.) Neocons have always claimed that narcissism, not ideology, inspired the rebelliousness of Dylan's generation. Dylan, the most inward looking of musicians, a selfish genius, gives that claim credence.

Other musicians pander to their public. Dylan has built a career designed to satisfy no one but himself. In 1965, for example, Dylan went electric, abandoning folk's soft sound, earnest politics, and rabidly loyal fans. When some pop musicians turned to psychedelia in the late '60s, this one stripped his songs down and played basic American country. A decade later, at a time of high hedonism, he found Jesus and composed gospel music. Dylan, who modeled himself on James Dean, spent a vast amount of time away from music trying to build a movie career—despite a total absence of acting charisma.

Throughout his career, Dylan has intentionally frustrated fans by deconstructing his golden oldies. When he plays his hits in concerts, Dylan often twists them, garbling their lyrics and sand-blasting their melodies into strange new creations. (Anyone who has attended a Dylan show in the past 30 years knows the feeling: He plays a song you've always loved, and you can't even recognize it. "That was 'Tangled Up in Blue'?")

Dylan got bad, but he never got stale. His constant reinvention and his constant touring saved him from rock geezerhood. If you go to a Rolling Stones or Eagles concert—and I strongly advise against it—three-quarters of the crowd will be paunchy baby boomers reliving their glory days. They'll sing along to 35-year-old songs performed exactly as they were 35 years ago. But Dylan has been touring practically nonstop since 1988, winning over an entire generation of fans to his music (both new and old). America may be waxing nostalgic over Dylan, but there has never been a musician less concerned with nostalgia.

In an age when celebrities expose themselves promiscuously, Dylan rejects public self-revelation. Is there any star about whom we know less? It's not that Dylan's invisible: He plays 150 concerts a year, and he does occasional interviews. But he says little about his music and nothing about his life. His marriage, his divorce, his personal life: All are ciphers in the public consciousness. Even his memoir is opaque: It's full of wit, and great stories, and superb character sketches, but it's oddly short of actual information about Dylan himself and virtually free of private revelations.

(He has mellowed slightly since his younger days, when he took pleasure in torturing the press.

Reporter: What do you do with your money?

Dylan: I wear it.

Another reporter: What are your songs about?

Dylan: Some of my songs are about four minutes, some are about five minutes and some, believe it or not, are about 11 or 12.)

And Dylan never schmoozed much within the music business. His failure to win Grammies during the '60s was hardly a surprise. The Grammies have always trailed hipness by a decade or more.

In the mid-'60s, when Dylan was at his peak, Herb Alpert was winning Album of the Year awards. Recently, the Grammies have become more current by adding categories, and they have begun to repay artists for years of neglect. Dylan probably won't reinvent himself again. He said recently that songs don't come to him easily anymore: *Time Out of Mind* and *Love and Theft* sound more like a return to something old and comfortable rather than progress to something new and strange.

And even if Dylan does have another transformation within him, his voice may not. Opera singers who take care of their voices can perform only into their sixties. Dylan is in his mid-60s, and his voice—ripped by drugs, alcohol, and cigarettes and never that good to begin with—is much older. Alex Ross called *Time Out of Mind* "the first great rock album of old age" in part because Dylan managed to sing around his weak voice. His range, already narrow, will soon be just a bleat. But better to go out bleating "Not Dark Yet" than croaking through "Blowin' in the Wind" for the 10,000th time.

The MacArthur Geniuses

How to become one of them.

BY DAVID PLOTZ

WHEN PETER HAYES LEARNED that he had won a $500,000 MacArthur genius grant in 2000, he was stunned: It's "like being hit by a Mack truck. . . . It's a little disorienting," he told the *San Francisco Chronicle*. Hayes shouldn't have been too disoriented. It would have been surprising if he hadn't collected a MacArthur. He helps North Korea develop windmills as an alternative to nuclear power. He takes underprivileged kids sailing in San Francisco Bay during his free time. And he lives in Berkeley, Calif., where you can't buy a latte without meeting a MacArthur-stamped brainiac.

Since 1981, the John D. and Catherine T. MacArthur Foundation has awarded more than 700 "fellowships" worth $250 million to Americans "who show exceptional merit and promise for continued and enhanced creative work." (The foundation detests the word "genius" because it "connotes a singular characteristic of intellectual prowess.") The fellowship is a no-strings-attached grant: Winners get $100,000 a year for five years. MacArthur calls the cash a gift of time, because it frees winners from financial constraints on their art, science, or activism. (The $5 billion foundation is the estate of John D. MacArthur, a skinflint who became the second-richest American by selling cut-rate insurance through the mail. His son Rod grabbed control of the trust after John's 1978 death and pushed the genius project.)

The MacArthur has become the United States' most famous philanthropy project not because it rewards stellar people—though it does—but because it's mysterious. Several hundred talent scouts, whose identities are secret, suggest nominees to the selection committee. The committee, whose members are also secret, covertly gathers dossiers on the nominees and selects two-dozen-odd winners. In a nation where self-promotion is a constitutional right, the MacArthur is endlessly frustrating: You can't nominate yourself, you can't nominate a friend, you can't lobby for it if you are nominated. What's an unappreciated genius to do?

Don't fear, the MacArthur is less cryptic than it seems. It can be gamed. You may not be able to guarantee yourself half-a-million bucks and a reputation for brilliance, but you can certainly improve your odds. Here's a how-to guide for becoming a certifiable genius.

Rule No. 1: Live in New York or San Francisco. New Yorkers and San Franciscans act like they're the most interesting people in the world. MacArthur agrees with them. Fully one-sixth of all MacArthurs live in Manhattan, and nearly as many live in the Bay Area.

No matter what, don't live in the South. Southerners rarely qualify as geniuses unless they're sensitive writers or colorful advocates for the poor. (Your typical Southern winner is 2000 fellow Samuel Mockbee, an Auburn professor who builds houses for poor Alabamans out of old tires and hay bales.) The Great Plains and Rockies are equally inhospitable to genius: You're unlikely to win unless you've started a bank or college on an Indian reservation. Stick to the Northeast and the West Coast.

Rule No. 2: Be a professor. Specifically, be a professor at Harvard or Stanford, where they hand out MacArthurs like candy. If you're a humanities professor, choose Harvard (which has 40 MacArthurs) or University of California, Berkeley (which has 27). Hard scientists should land a job at Stanford (27) or Princeton

(24). Physicists at one of those two universities seem to win MacArthurs more easily than tenure. In a pinch, University of Chicago, University of Michigan, Columbia, and New York University are acceptable backups, but avoid Yale! It's got only eight geniuses. You'd be better off with Bard College, whose tiny faculty has won five MacArthurs. (As Harvard grads have always suspected, Yale is approximately one-fifth as good as Harvard.)

But it's not enough to be a professor. You also must choose the right specialty. Ancient civilizations win MacArthurs. Revisionist scholars of classical Greece do well, and MacArthur has identified not one, but two geniuses who decipher ancient Mayan glyphs, a third who deciphers ancient Andean knotted mnemonic devices (whatever they may be), and a fourth who rescues damaged papyrus texts. Literature, philosophy, and history all win plenty of MacArthurs. Economics is unpromising, unless you study something odd. 2000 winner Matthew Rabin, for example, analyzes the economic implications of procrastination, while 2002 champ Sendhil Mullainathan studies willpower (which, come to think of it, is the same as studying procrastination). Physics, math, and computer science are beloved of MacArthur. Chemistry is a lost cause. Environmentalism is a sure winner. Biologists should study evolution, dinosaurs, or primates, and little else.

Rule No. 3: If you don't want to teach college, make art. Preferably in New York: One in 10 MacArthurs is a writer, choreographer, artist, musician, or director in New York City. Again, pick the right specialty. Be a poet or a choreographer. Novelists have been coming on strong in the past few years, while painters and film directors seem underrepresented. Among musicians, bluegrass, ragtime, and jazz are good, and free jazz is even better. Needless to say, no matter what kind of artist you are, be avant-garde.

Rule No. 4: Do not, under any circumstances, work for the government or the private sector. This cannot be stressed enough. Many MacArthur geniuses advocate government activism, but all fellows assiduously avoid public service. I found only two

MacArthur winners from the public sector, small-town mayor Unita Blackwell and then–Congressional Budget Office director Alice Rivlin. Similarly, geniuses should not soil themselves with earning a profit. It's fine to run a nonprofit that helps disadvantaged people start their own businesses, but almost no MacArthurs run or work for profit-seeking corporations.

Rule No. 5: Upset conventional wisdom. You don't have to be right, but you must be provocative. It's not enough to study quantum physics. You must, like 1999 winner Eva Silverstein, "question the fundamentals of quantum physics." MacArthur honored the classicist who reinterpreted the Parthenon friezes as a human sacrifice and the paleontologist who says that Tyrannosaurus Rex ate carrion rather than hunted. If you're a mathematician, set yourself one of math's great insoluble problems: MacArthur knighted Andrew Wiles for cracking Fermat's Theorem and Michael Freedman for proving the four-dimensional case of Poincare's Conjecture.

The best kind of provocation is a doomsday theory. MacArthur adores folks who foresee the end of the world, especially if that end is caused by Western avarice or stupidity. MacArthur has blessed Paul "Population Explosion" Ehrlich; Richard Turco, who popularized the idea of nuclear winter; and several scientists who have sounded warnings about global warming.

Rule No. 6: Be left-wing. MacArthur generally finds genius on the left. Only a handful of the 588 genies could be considered conservative. (Black community developer Robert Woodson is the most notable.) On the other hand, four *Dissent* editorial board members have won the MacArthur, according to the *American Spectator*. The foundation likes artists who campaign for racial minorities and the needy. Alfredo Jaar, a 2000 winner, creates art that "focuses on injustices around the world—poverty, exploitation, genocide." 2001 fellow Julie Su protects undocumented immigrant garment workers. 2005 MacArthur Aaron Dworkin seeks to increase the number of minorities in classical music. 1997 winner

Kara Walker constructs silhouettes about racial and sexual exploitation. 2000 fellow David Isay produces brilliant radio documentaries about the lives of poor Americans. The foundation favors activists who fight for low-income housing, disability rights, and racial justice. Libertarians, religious conservatives, and free marketeers are never geniuses. MacArthur routinely consecrates the causes célèbres of the left, from sex discrimination to right-wing human rights abuses in Central America (see: Mark Danner, Tina Rosenberg, and Alma Guillermoprieto).

The MacArthur's reliable support of left-wing causes makes it fun to guess future winners. My bets: 1) someone who lobbies to protect privacy in an age of corporate and government surveillance (maybe Jerry Berman from the Center for Democracy and Technology?) and 2) someone who thinks nanotechnology will turn us all into grey goo.

Rule No. 7: Be slightly, but not dangerously, quirky. MacArthur favors the eccentric choice over the ordinary. Economist Rabin wears tie-dyes, listens to Abba, and has Johnny Depp posters all over his office wall. David Stuart won when he was an 18-year-old prodigy. Recluse Thomas Pynchon took a MacArthur; social butterfly John Updike has not. And it surely helped Seattle "sound sculptor" Trimpin that he goes by only one name.

All the rules suggest that the perfect MacArthur genius is still out there: a one-named Berkeley professor who choreographs interpretative jazz dances about how genetically modified food will destroy humanity.

ANIMALS WE HATE

Giant Pandas

Black and White and Dumb All Over

BY DAVID PLOTZ

THE NATION'S CAPITAL has been captured by pandas again. Tickets to see the cub Tai Shan and his parents Mei Xiang and Tian Tian are the hottest commodity in town. Children are being bussed in to gaze upon the pandas; Adults who should know better stand outside the fence for hours and drool at the slightest twitch of fur. They shouldn't get too used to the cub: The Chinese government will take back Tai Shan when he turns two, and there are only four years left on the 10-year lease signed in 2000 for the parents. When they are sent back to China, no doubt the National Zoo will expand the trade deficit (and the federal deficit) again by renting another pair of black-and-whites, so the cycle of googling and gushing can continue.

All over the country, zoos are in the thrall of these semi-bears, and generation after generation of kids is being indoctrinated into the panda cult. Has there ever been so much goodwill wasted on a creature that deserved it less?

I have long been a victim of the panda people. I arrived in Washington in late 1970 as a six-month-old infant. A year later, Hsing-Hsing and Ling-Ling arrived at the National Zoo, a gift from Mao's China to the United States. I think of this as the opening round in the U.S.-China trade war—the first effort by the Chinese to win over American consumers with an attractive but incredibly shoddy product. As a child, I took more field trips and family outings than I can count to visit the panda cellmates. As an adult, I have lived next door to the zoo for the past decade, and witnessed the death of Hsing-Hsing (Ling-Ling died in 1992), the arrival of the new pandas, the Herculean efforts to mate them, and the birth of the cub. So I speak from the heart when I say: Let's get rid of them, forever.

Pandas drive otherwise reasonable people barking mad. At the time of his death, Hsing-Hsing was the most famous animal in the world. More than 60 million people had visited him during his life sentence at the zoo. Pandaphilia has turned the *Washington Post* into the zoo's own propaganda rag. Hsing-Hsing "enchanted" and "enthralled" visitors. He was "sweet-natured"—the most "cuddly" and adorable of all creatures. "The world needs all the teddy bears it can get," declared the paper. I would hazard that the *Post* devoted more column inches to the new panda cub than to the decision to go to war in Iraq.

George Schaller, a leading panda biologist, describes giant pandas as perfectly symbolic animals. With their lovely fur, clumsy movements, and goofy faces, they seem the embodiment of innocence, childishness, and vulnerability. This is also the public image so carefully cultivated for them by endangered-species activists. But behind the pretty face lurks, well, a bore. The idea that pandas are sweet and genial is ridiculous. Pandas are not ill-natured. They are worse: They are no-natured. Drearier animals you cannot imagine. They are highly anti-social, detesting interaction with other pandas and people. In all my treks to the pandas' cell and yard, I have never once seen them be playful or affectionate or active or even violent. Compared to almost any other animal in the zoo—apes, big cats, seals, prairie dogs, snakes—the pandas were a drag. They led a life of unparalleled tedium. Pandas are Mother Nature's couch potatoes. They are staggeringly lazy, so slothful they avoid climbing trees because it's too tiring. Their entire lives are spent eating bamboo and sleeping. (Not that there is anything wrong with eating and sleeping—I would like to spend my own life that way—just don't call it endearing.)

Pandas are not simply dull. They are also unpleasant. Confinement depresses zoo animals, and pandas are no exception, behaving more like kooks than teddy bears. The last pair grew nuttier and nuttier the longer they were in captivity (which may be why the new pandas are limited to 10-year leases). Ling-Ling, unprovoked, assaulted one of her keepers and gnawed on his ankle. The animals' decadelong attempt to mate was played as comic opera, but it was much darker. At first Hsing-Hsing failed to inseminate Ling-Ling because he tried to mate with her ear and her arm. Then the zoo imported a male panda from the London Zoo to mate with Ling-Ling. He mauled her instead. Eventually Hsing-Hsing got it right, and between 1983 and 1989, Ling-Ling bore five of his cubs. All of them died within days. One cub perished after Ling-Ling sat on it. Another seems to have been killed by a urinary tract infection acquired from Ling-Ling. Keepers believe Ling-Ling infected herself by sticking bamboo and carrots up her urinary tract, surely neurotic behavior. (At least Mei Xiang and Tian Tian can do this fundamental right.)

When the pandas get sent back to China, the zoo should resist the public pressure to replace them with the latest model—at $10 million a pair. Instead, they should leave the pandas to their tedious bamboo lives and buy a few extra seals and kangaroos instead.

And here's the great part: No one needs to know that there's no new panda. When Hsing Hsing died in 1999, the Smithsonian had him stuffed. The zoo could just pull the taxidermed bear out of storage, jam a rod of bamboo in his paws, and prop him up in his old cage. I doubt that anyone would notice the difference.

Salmon

Swimming downstream.

BY BRYAN CURTIS

SALMON IS A MERCILESSLY AGREEABLE FISH. It can accommodate any sauce and be slipped noiselessly into almost any ceviche. It has more flavor than cod, yet it is just retiring enough to be served aboard an airplane, at a wedding reception, or wherever else bland cuisine reigns. If you had never tried seafood, you would probably love salmon. (Correlative theory: If you have never tried sushi, you would probably love salmon sushi.) Fifteen years after it exploded in the American and Japanese markets, fresh salmon still sells at a brisk clip, often trailing only shellfish and tuna. In Seattle, where I lived for a time, salmon had become the local mascot, and the citizenry regarded it with a mixture of pride and resignation. "I'll have the salmon!" was the civic motto, and those who failed to comply with enthusiasm were pelted with muesli.

These days, however, there's a numb and slightly uneasy feeling when you see a lump of the pink fish dumped on your plate. The feeling, the opposite of the salmon worship of the late 1980s, is more like salmon fatigue—an abiding sense that the wonder fish has become déclassé. Ordering salmon in a seafood restaurant produces a mild feeling of shame, the kind of embarrassment one feels when a dinner companion requests spaghetti bolognese at an Italian eatery or pad thai at a Thai joint. A survey of a few elite New York chefs confirms this suspicion. "It's pretty much passé," says Dan Barber, owner of the chic Greenwich Village restaurant Blue Hill. What happened?

It's fitting that salmon should endure an identity crisis. Throughout its long history—Ken Schultz's *Fishing Encyclopedia* calls Atlantic salmon "possibly the most important single species of fish in a historical and an economic sense"—the salmon has been dogged by issues of class. Salmon was once an ornament of the elite, enjoyed by Roman emperors and singled out for conservation in the Magna Carta. It was a consuming passion of European royals, from King George IV's feasting on the "last" salmon of the Thames in 1832 to the Queen Mother's salmon-fishing hobby a century later. Yet salmon has an equally compelling history as a food of the underclasses. British noblemen fed so much salmon to their servants in the 1600s that the vassals stumped for a law that limited salmon rations to three per week. Lox (from *lachs*, the German word for salmon) was a favorite of European Jews who crowded into New York's Lower East Side at the turn of the century; they bought the cheap salmon that trundled in from the Pacific Ocean by rail. As it cured in tenements, lox became a symbol of the Jewish immigrant experience—a shoestring delicacy, a symbol of a newfound freedom and hope.

In the late 1980s, salmon shed both its royal and prole roots and became the go-to fish of the American middle class. Health is the most oft-cited reason for salmon's rise: It comes chocked full of heart-healthy omega-3 fatty acids. But salmon also suits the peculiarities of the American diner. For example, its serving size—a thick steak about the size of a chicken breast—fits the continental diner's lust for gargantuan portions. The salmon also satisfies the American urge to romanticize dinner. Since the days of Pliny the Elder, every time a salmon has swum upstream it has elicited a paean to its bravery and nobility. Typical example (from the enthusiasts at Whats CookingAmerica.net): "They will leap over any obstacle in their way, such as braving dams and waterfalls, hurling [themselves] many feet out of the water until [they] surmount the obstacle or die of exhaustion in the attempt; there is no turning back." Nothing quite so stirring has ever been written about a monkfish.

So why has salmon's star begun to fade? First, the fish has faced a nonstop barrage of bad press. Most of it has targeted the farm-raised salmon, a sad creature of "aquaculture" that is raised in offshore cages and bathed in pink dye. (Wild salmon obtain their pink color by eating shellfish.) Aquaculture often pollutes oceans and chokes salmon with contaminants. A 2004 report in *Science* found some farm-raised salmon so hepped up on PCBs and dioxins that the authors recommend eating it no more than once a month. Other studies discovered salmon with trace amounts—and here direct quotation is necessary—of an "industrial-strength fire retardant" and a "Chlamydia-like bacterium." At this news, upscale diners retreated to the more expensive wild salmon breeds. Then, in April 2005, the *New York Times* revealed that a half-dozen of New York's finer fish markets claiming to be selling wild salmon were actually purveying its farm-raised counterpart, sending the denizens of the Upper West Side into collective shock.

The rise of other upwardly mobile fish has also hurt the salmon. First came the Patagonian toothfish, whose name was changed to the more appealing "Chilean sea bass," lest anyone confuse it with Augusto Pinochet. By the late 1990s, the Chilean sea bass had been overfished into scarcity; in any case, it seems far too rarefied to best the salmon. These days, fishmongers lay better odds on tilapia, the latest sharpie from Latin America. Already claiming to be the sixth most-popular fish in the United States, tilapia stands as the anti-salmon—farm-raised with less threat to fish and ecosystem. Where salmon can boast of Roman bona fides, tilapia can claim that it was fished from the Sea of Galilee and, according to some historians, served at the Last Supper. Matt Hovey, a fishmonger at Wild Edibles in New York, pronounces tilapia the "white-meat chicken of seafood"—that is, even more aggressively banal than its pink cousin.

Salmon also has a branding problem. When it boomed in the late 1980s, it was positioned at the leading edge of the health-food craze, just as the specter of heart disease was in full throttle and the American middle class was making a reluctant lurch from red meat to fish. For many, salmon was a first such step—because it came as a "steak" instead of a fillet; because it was less fishy than some of the alternatives. Sadly, this is the source of salmon's lament today. Salmon has been irrevocably branded as a "starter fish"—seafood training wheels—and for many that's where its image has remained frozen ever since. As the middle-class palate has grown more sophisticated and Americans have begun to embrace all manner of nouveau fishes—Arctic char, steelhead—salmon suddenly seems charmingly retrograde: the bran muffin of fish.

Another theory: As we have outgrown salmon, it has also outgrown us. Salmon has gone upscale. Note, for example, the proliferation of boutique salmon "brands" that fetch absurd prices from the high-end fish markets. (For a time, wild Alaskan King moved for more than $25 a pound.) The demand for wild salmon is so intense that some finer restaurants serve it only for a few weeks, during the salmon runs. Julian Niccolini, the co-owner of New York's Four Seasons restaurant and a reliable tastemaker for the super-rich, describes an uptick in salmon connoisseurship. Four Seasons diners, it seems, have begun requesting the wild salmon breeds by name. On a recent occasion, Niccolini even noticed a diner taking his salmon medium rare. "Can you imagine that?" Niccolini told me, with wilting Italian hauteur. "After so many years of being grilled to death, of being baked to death, the customers are finally getting it." The upper-tier restaurant would be a fitting destination for the salmon, the fish that spends its life swimming upstream.

DEAD, BUT WON'T GO AWAY

Lewis and Clark

Stop celebrating. They don't matter.

BY DAVID PLOTZ

THE AMERICAN INFATUATION with Lewis and Clark grows more fervent with every passing year. The adventurers have become our Extreme Founding Fathers, as essential to American history as George Washington and Thomas Jefferson but a lot more fun. The Lewis and Clark bicentennial celebration, a 15-state pageant, drew tens of millions of tourists to the Lewis and Clark trail between 2003 and 2006.

Bookstores have been stuffed with Lewis and Clark volumes since the publication of Stephen Ambrose's in 1996. There are scores of trail guides, multivolume editions of the explorers' journals, a dozen books about Sacagawea, three histories of Fort Clatsop, a Lewis and Clark cookbook, and at least three books about Meriwether Lewis' dog, Seaman.

Our Lewis and Clark have something for everyone—a catalog of 21st-century virtues. They're multicultural: An Indian woman, French-Indians, French-Canadians, and a black slave all contributed to the expedition's success. They're environmental: Lewis and Clark kept prodigious records of plants and animals and were enthralled by the vast, mysterious landscape they traveled through. They're tolerant: They didn't kill Indians (much) but did negotiate with them. They're patriotic: They discovered new land so the United States could grow into a great nation. Lewis and

Clark, it's claimed, opened the West and launched the American empire.

Except they didn't. "If Lewis and Clark had died on the trail, it wouldn't have mattered a bit," says Notre Dame University historian Thomas Slaughter, author of *Exploring Lewis and Clark: Reflections on Men and Wilderness*.

Like the moon landing, the Lewis and Clark expedition was inspiring, poetic, metaphorical, and ultimately insignificant. First of all, Lewis and Clark were not first of all. The members of the Corps of Discovery were not the first people to see the land they traveled. Indians had been everywhere, of course, but the corps members were not even the first whites. Trappers and traders had covered the land before them, and though Lewis and Clark may have been the first whites to cross the Rockies in the United States, explorer Alexander MacKenzie had traversed the Canadian Rockies a decade before them.

After the celebration of their safe return, Lewis and Clark quickly sank into obscurity, and for good reason. They failed at their primary mission. Jefferson had dispatched them to find a water route across the continent—the fabled Northwest Passage—but they discovered that water transport from coast to coast was impossible. Jefferson, chagrined, never bragged much about the expedition he had fathered.

Not discovering something that didn't exist was hardly Lewis and Clark's fault, but the expedition also failed in a much more important way. It produced nothing useful. Meriwether Lewis was supposed to distill his notes into a gripping narrative, but he had writer's block and killed himself in 1809 without ever writing a word. The captains' journals weren't published until almost 10 years after the duo's return; only 1,400 copies were printed, they appeared when the country was distracted by the War of 1812, and they had no impact. The narrative was well-told, but it ignored the most valuable information collected by Lewis and Clark: their mountains of scientific and anthropological data about the plants, animals, and Indians of the West. That material wasn't published for a century, long after it could have helped pioneers.

Lewis and Clark didn't matter for other reasons. At the time of the journey, the Corps of Discovery "leapfrogged Americans' concerns," says American University historian Andrew Lewis (no relation to Meriwether). "They were exploring the far Missouri at a time when the frontier was the Ohio River. They were irrelevant."

When the country did start catching up, decades later, the Lewis and Clark route didn't help. William Clark told President Jefferson that they had discovered the best route across the continent, but he could hardly have been more wrong. Lewis and Clark took the Missouri through Kansas, Iowa, Nebraska, the Dakotas, and Montana before crossing the Rockies in Northern Idaho. Their route was way too far north to be practical. No one could follow it. Other explorers located better, southerly shortcuts across the Continental Divide, and that's where Western settlers went. Lewis and Clark aficionados delight today in the unspoiled scenery along the trail. The reason the trail remains scenic and unspoiled is that it was so useless.

In a few years, Lewis and Clark disappeared from the American imagination and the American project. Lewis was dead, and Clark spent the rest of his life on the frontier, supervising relations with Indians—an important job, but not one that gave him any say over government policy. Meanwhile, other daredevils captured the popular fancy, especially during the great wave of exploration in the mid–19th century. John C. Frémont enthralled the country with his bold Western trips. John Wesley Powell—the one-armed Civil War veteran—made his name by rafting the Colorado River through the Grand Canyon. The midcentury explorers provided information that was vastly more productive than anything Lewis and Clark offered.

By the late 19th century, Lewis and Clark were negligible figures. They weren't found in textbooks, according to the University of Tulsa's James Ronda, a leading scholar of the expedition. Americans didn't hearken back to the adventure. It was so unimportant that Henry Adams could dismiss it in no time flat in his history of the Jefferson administration as having "added little to the stock of science and wealth."

The first Lewis and Clark revival occurred at the turn of the 20th century, when the journals were published again after an 80-year hiatus. Americans were remembering the trip only after the West had been settled, the Indians had been wiped out, and the frontier closed. During the years that the empire was actually being built, at the time of settlement and conquest, Americans hadn't cared at all about Lewis and Clark.

After World War I, says Ronda, the expedition was ignored again. University of Texas historian William Goetzmann says that when he was writing his Pulitzer-Prize–winning *Exploration and Empire: The Explorer and the Scientist in the Winning of the American West* in the mid-'60s, he wasn't even going to include Lewis and Clark, but "my publisher talked me into it."

But by the late '60s, Americans had rediscovered Lewis and Clark, and their fervor has not flagged since. The creation of the 3,700-mile Lewis and Clark National Historic Trail in 1978 made the story accessible in a way that history rarely is. Millions of people have followed Lewis and Clark's footsteps and oar-swings since the trail opened. Ambrose's book attracted tens of thousands of new fans to the tale. The expedition's various appeal—ecological, patriotic, diverse, literary, thrill-seeking—gives it traction. More and more Americans read directly from the captains' journals, whose blunt, direct, and oddly beautiful language makes the story live. And the United States, as Ronda notes, is a country that loves road stories, and there is none more vivid or exciting than Lewis and Clark's.

But our fascination with Lewis and Clark is much more about us than about them. The expedition is a useful American mythology: How a pair of hardy souls and their happy-go-lucky multiculti flotilla discovered Eden, befriended the Indian, and invented the

American West. The myth of Lewis and Clark papers over the grittier story of how the United States conquered the land, tribe by slaughtered, betrayed tribe.

Lewis and Clark didn't give Americans any of the tools they required to settle the continent—not new technology, not a popular narrative, not a good route, not arable land. It didn't matter. Nineteenth-century pioneers were bound to take the great West, with or without Lewis and Clark. Their own greed, ambition, bravery, and desperation guaranteed it. They did not need Lewis and Clark to conquer and build the West. But we do need Lewis and Clark to justify having done it.

St. Patrick

No snakes. No shamrocks. Just the facts.

BY DAVID PLOTZ

ON MARCH 17, WE RAISE A GLASS of warm green beer to a fine fellow, the Irishman who didn't rid the land of snakes, didn't compare the Trinity to the shamrock, and wasn't even Irish. St. Patrick, who died 1,513, 1,545, or 1,546 years ago today—depending on which unreliable source you want to believe—has been adorned with centuries of Irish blarney. Innumerable folk tales recount how he faced down kings, negotiated with God, tricked and slaughtered Ireland's reptiles.

The facts about St. Patrick are few. Most derive from the two documents he probably wrote, the autobiographical *Confession* and the indignant *Letter* to a slave-taking marauder named Coroticus. Patrick was born in Britain, probably in Wales, around 385 A.D. His father was a Roman official. When Patrick was 16, seafaring raiders captured him, carried him to Ireland, and sold him into slavery. The Christian Patrick spent six lonely years herding sheep and, according to him, praying 100 times a day. In a dream, God told him to escape. He returned home, where he had another vision in which the Irish people begged him to return and minister to them: "We ask thee, boy, come and walk among us once more," he recalls in the *Confession*. He studied for the priesthood in France, then made his way back to Ireland.

He spent his last 30 years there, baptizing pagans, ordaining priests, and founding churches and monasteries. His persuasive powers must have been astounding: Ireland fully converted to Christianity within 200 years and was the only country in Europe to Christianize peacefully. Patrick's Christian conversion ended slavery, human sacrifice, and most intertribal warfare in Ireland. (He did not banish the snakes: Ireland never had any. Scholars now consider snakes a metaphor for the serpent of paganism. Nor did he invent the Shamrock Trinity. That was an 18th-century fabrication.)

According to Thomas Cahill, author of *How the Irish Saved Civilization*, Paddy's influence extended far beyond his adopted land. Cahill's book, which could just as well be titled *How St. Patrick Saved Civilization*, contends that Patrick's conversion of Ireland allowed Western learning to survive the Dark Ages. Ireland pacified and churchified as the rest of Europe crumbled. Patrick's monasteries copied and preserved classical texts. Later, Irish monks returned this knowledge to Europe by establishing monasteries in England, Germany, France, Switzerland, and Italy.

The Irish have celebrated their patron saint with a quiet religious holiday for centuries, perhaps more than 1,000 years. It took the United States to turn St. Patrick's Day into a boozy spectacle. Irish immigrants first celebrated it in Boston in 1737 and first paraded in New York in 1762. By the late 19th century, the St. Patrick's Day parade had become a way for Irish-Americans to flaunt their numerical and political might. It retains this role today.

The scarcity of facts about St. Patrick's life has made him a dress-up doll: Anyone can create his own St. Patrick. Ireland's Catholics and Protestants, who have long feuded over him, each have built a St. Patrick in their own image. Catholics cherish Paddy as the father of Catholic Ireland. They say that Patrick was consecrated as a bishop and that the pope himself sent him to convert the heathen Irish. (Evidence is sketchy about both the bishop and pope claims.) One of the most popular Irish Catholic stories holds that Patrick bargained with God and got the Big Fella to promise that Ireland would remain Catholic and free.

Ireland's Protestant minority, by contrast, denies that Patrick was a bishop or that he was sent by Rome. They depict him as anti–Roman Catholic and credit him with inventing a distinctly Celtic church, with its own homegrown symbols and practices. He is an Irish hero, not a Catholic one.

Outside Ireland, too, Patrick has been freely reinterpreted. Evangelical Protestants claim him as one of their own. After all, he read his Bible, and his faith came to him in visions. Biblical inspiration and personal revelation are Protestant hallmarks. Utah newspapers emphasize that Patrick was a missionary sent overseas to convert the ungodly, an image that resonates in Mormon country. New Age Christians revere Patrick as a virtual patron saint. Patrick co-opted Druid symbols in order to undermine the rival religion, fusing nature and magic with Christian practice. The Irish placed a sun at the center of their cross. "St. Patrick's Breastplate," Patrick's famous prayer (which he certainly did not write), invokes the power of the sun, moon, rocks, and wind, as well as God. (This is what is called "Erin go hoo-ha.")

Patrick has even been enlisted in the gay rights cause. For a decade, gay and lesbian Irish-Americans have sought permission to march in New York's St. Patrick's Day Parade, and for a decade they have lost in court. Cahill, among others, has allied Patrick with gays and lesbians. Cahill's Patrick is a muscular progressive. He was a proto-feminist who valued women in an age when the church ignored them. He always sided with the downtrodden and the excluded, whether they were slaves or the pagan Irish. If Patrick were around today, Cahill says, he would join the gay marchers.

Here comes another Patrick. The latest popular culture Paddy is the hero of the TV movie *St. Patrick*. This small-screen Patrick is mostly drawn from the historical record, but the producers added one new storyline. The English parent church demands that Patrick collect its church taxes in Ireland. Patrick rebels and risks excommunication by the British bishop. The fearless colonist leads a tax revolt against the villainous English. We Americans, like everyone else, think St. Patrick is one of us.

Frank Sinatra

Can even Death stop Ol' Blue Eyes?

BY DAVID PLOTZ

FRANK SINATRA HAS ALWAYS SAID that "dyin' is a pain in the ass," but it hasn't been so bad. Sinatra took his limo ride to the Big Casino in 1998, but dead, as living, the Chairman of the Board is right where he's always liked to be: at the center of attention. Unlike fellow crooners (Tony Bennett, Barry Manilow, etc.), Sinatra has transcended irony and avoided kitsch. Music critics and the record-buying public, who don't agree about much, agree that Sinatra is the greatest popular singer in American history.

Sinatra has ascended to a state of perpetual cool. This actually began in the '90s, during the last of many rediscoveries of Sinatra, and never ended. His 1993 *Duets* album—in which he sings his greatest hits with pop stars such as Luther Vandross and U2's Bono—sold upwards of 3 million copies in the United States, far more than any of his earlier recordings. Swingers paid slavish tribute to Sinatra lounge culture. Sinatraism became the house religion at men's magazines such as *Esquire*. The pinnacle of this was *The Way You Wear Your Hat: Frank Sinatra and the Lost Art of Livin'*, a 1997 book by *Esquire*'s Bill Zehme, which instructed on swaggers, cocktails, $100 tips, street fights, and seductions. (All should be frequent.) This cocky, swinging guy is our Sinatra. His misogyny and promiscuity have been recast as healthy libido, his Mafia ties and thuggery as macho. He's a man's man. How could you not admire a fellow who bedded Lana Turner, Ava Gardner, Mia Farrow, Anita Ekberg, Marlene Dietrich, and Marilyn Monroe?

But today's Sinatraism is very different from the Sinatra worship of the past. Sinatra rose and fell as a teen idol in the '40s, then returned to stardom in the early '50s. Between 1953 and the mid-'60s, he made his best records, scored most of his biggest *Billboard* hits, gave his finest film performances (*The Manchurian Candidate* and *From Here to Eternity*, for which he won an Academy Award), and exerted the greatest political and cultural influence. (Some particularly enthusiastic, daft Sinatra fans credit him with Kennedy's 1960 election victory, claiming that Sinatra helped line up the Mob behind JFK.)

Since that peak, Sinatra nostalgia has been a cottage industry of American culture. Every few years, Sinatra is "rediscovered." Sinatra himself doesn't change; what changes is the way we choose to perceive him. He's a national Rorschach test: America periodically concocts a new Sinatra to fit the Zeitgeist.

Consider the Sinatra revival of the early '70s. He came back as a Me Generation icon, the Rat Packer reincarnated as an individualist. His late '60s albums, dismissed as lame attempts to ape rock when they debuted, were now applauded for their courageous, free-spirit experimentalism. Critics harked back to his original popularity in the '40s, noting that Sinatra had helped to end the Big Band era and usher in the age of the individual star. His signature song, after all, was "My Way."

When punk broke in the late '70s, Sinatra was reborn again—this time as Proto-Punk, popular music's first great rebel. Sinatra had been one of the first artists to start his own record label (Reprise, in 1961): This was recognized in the late '70s as proof of his artistic integrity and a kick in the smug face of corporate music. His brawling and boozing in the '50s presaged the punks' brawling and boozing in the '70s. Even Sinatra's Mob ties supposedly demonstrated his flouting of authority. The Sex Pistols' Sid Vicious recorded "My Way," a bizarre combination of homage and scorn.

His next incarnation: Reaganite. Through the '80s, Sinatra palled around with Ron, Nancy, and his usual crew of sycophants. The punk became Ol' Blue Eyes. For Reaganites, Sinatra symbolized all that was once right about America (and would be again after a few years of supply-side economics): classy music, machismo, bonhomie, and good times. (The right's embrace of Sinatra inspired the oddest chapter in the Sinatra cycle: a counterclaim by the left. *The New Republic* and others tried to redeem Sinatra for liberals, advertising his early support of civil rights, his assistance to black musicians before such help became fashionable, his opposition to McCarthyism, and his failed attempt to break the Hollywood Communist blacklist.)

There's one other Sinatra phenomenon that keeps repeating itself: dirt. In the '60s and '70s, rumors of Sinatra's Mob ties were family entertainment. In 1986, Kitty Kelley's dishy biography, *His Way*, confirmed most of the nasty gossip about his love life. *Sinatra: Behind the Legend*, a warts-and-all (and-more-warts) biography, offered salacious details about Frank's long affair with Monroe, other extracurricular activities, and an aborted Mob hit on him. Mafia boss Sam Giancana allegedly canceled the hit after hearing a Sinatra album.

Oscar Wilde

Why the 19th century insurgent has made a 21st century comeback.

BY DAVID PLOTZ

EVEN OSCAR WILDE, perhaps the greatest of all self-promoters, couldn't fault the hype job being done for him these days. He's gotten a biopic, at least four major new plays (notably *The Judas Kiss*, about his doomed love affair with Lord Alfred Douglas), several one-man shows, and an opera. Bookstores have been glutted with mass-market Wildeana: *Oscar Wilde's Guide to Modern Living; Wilde the Irishman; The Oscar Wilde Reader; Andre* and *Oscar; Oscar Wilde* (by his son Vyvyan Holland); and *The Wilde Album* (by his grandson Merlin Holland). And as for Wilde's own work, there is the usual spate of theatrical productions, as well as a surfeit of films of his plays and novel.

Normally this kind of wretched historical excess should be deplored and stifled. But in Oscar Wilde, the celebrity culture has found a subject worthy of this superfluity, someone complicated and challenging enough to endure the excess and more. Wilde once wrote, "I was a man who stood in symbolic relation to the art and culture of my age." He is now a man who stands in symbolic relation to the art and culture of our age.

For most of 20th century, Wilde was simply a cartoon figure, a bon-moting smart aleck. "I can resist everything except temptation." Ha ha ha! "There is only one thing in the world worse than being talked about, and that is not being talked about." How droll,

Oscar, how very droll! Wilde said that he "summed up . . . all existence in an epigram." And that is exactly how he has been perceived—as the cool, cruel master of aphorism. His plays were produced and his quips were plagiarized, but he himself remained a one-dimensional figure in the popular culture.

That has changed during the last few years. The revival largely ignores the art for the sake of the man, recognizing that Wilde himself is at least as interesting as his one-liners. Requisite quote: "I put my genius into my life. I have put only my talent into my works."

So why is the man suddenly so popular? One reason is that this is an age of memoirs: Wilde, who self-consciously made his own life a work of art, is an evocative symbol for self-involved literature. The 100th anniversary of his imprisonment, trials, and death were occasions for outpourings of literary nostalgia. Wilde's combination of stylishness and tragedy lends itself perfectly to overcostumed, overwrought Merchant-Ivory-style drama.

But there are two more important reasons why this is a Wilde time: homosexuality and celebrity. The rise of gay studies and increasing acceptance of gay themes in popular culture have made a Wilde resurgence inevitable. Wilde's homosexuality was ignored for decades, then glossed over. When he was first claimed as a gay icon a generation ago, he was explained too simply as a martyr: A vicious British society destroyed him because it was too intolerant to accept homosexuality.

Today's Wilde provokes because he is not simple at all. In an era obsessed by identity, sexuality, and ambiguity, Wilde is one of the most puzzling cases. His life raises very modern questions about what homosexuality is and how much sexuality should define identity. Wilde is the "ur-homosexual," as scholars put it, yet he never saw himself as homosexual. In fact, it is only after his trials—and partly because of his trials—that people began to be classified as "homosexual" and "heterosexual." Wilde was not only not explicitly gay, he was happily married and the father of two children. He had sex with men infrequently, and only late in life.

To appreciate the complexity of his sexuality, consider the recent crop of Wilde plays: The *Judas Kiss* focuses on his love affair with a man, *Gross Indecency* focuses on his denials of his love affairs with men, and *The Secret Fall of Constance* Wilde focuses on his love affair with a woman. And yet, in a neat double backflip, Wilde is the source of some of our most enduring stereotypes about gays. His aestheticism, ironic wit, foppishness, and theatricality were widely imitated by young gay Englishmen in the first half of the century. These elements of the "Oxford manner" have endured as gay clichés.

Often called the first person famous for being famous, Wilde foreshadowed our modern celebrity obsession. At a time when realism and authenticity were in vogue, his life was a stylized performance designed to grab attention. In the early 1880s, before he had written anything worth mentioning, he made his name as London's great young aesthete. He mooned around the city carrying flowers and threw himself at the feet of actresses. Gilbert and Sullivan parodied him in *Patience*. He then got himself sent on an American lecture tour to drum up publicity for *Patience*'s U.S. production. He wore outrageous clothes and quipped his way across the States. (On arrival in New York: "I have nothing to declare except my genius.") His lectures about interior decorating were mobbed. He also milked his fame brilliantly after he'd achieved commercial success. He is undoubtedly the only canonical writer to endorse "Madame Fontaine's Bosom Beautifier," a breast-enlarging cream.

Just as his rise prefigured modern ideas about celebrity, so also did his fall. Wilde was the first mass-media celebrity criminal. The English gutter press, which was just developing a wide audience, whipped up public hatred toward him over his sex crimes and made him a pariah. Wilde scholars note his sex scandal is curiously evocative of Bill Clinton's: A spectacular public figure denies sexual indiscretion (in the face of overwhelming evidence) rather than risk challenging conventional morality.

One thing is missing from the Wilde revival: subversiveness. Wilde himself was endlessly transgressive, always finding a new way to jab Victorian complacency. He made vicious fun of the English bourgeoisie in plays such as *The Importance of Being Earnest*. The same bourgeoisie packed London houses and made him a fortune without realizing the joke was on them. It's impossible today to realize how shocking *The Picture of Dorian Gray* was to 1890s readers. And even Wilde's decision to endure prison rather than flee was a rebuke to England's inhumanity.

But there is very little wildness in today's Wilde. The books, plays, and movies are extremely couth, extremely respectable. Even 20 years ago, a movie about Wilde and his gay affair would have been considered remarkable: Today, it's a cliché. At the end of the 19th century, "gross indecency" could not even be described in court. Today, you can throw it on the screen and no one even notices. The challenge for Wilde lovers at the beginning of the 21st century is this: Find a way to appall.

L. Ron Hubbard

Scientology's esteemed founder.

BY MICHAEL CROWLEY

THE TABLOID DRAMA of Tom Cruise's madness and Katie Holmes' creepy path toward zombie bridedom and maternity has been a useful reminder of how truly strange Scientology is. By now those interested in the Cruise-Holmes saga may be passingly familiar with the church's creation myth, in which an evil, intergalactic warlord named Xenu kidnaps billions of alien life forms, chains them near Earth's volcanoes, and blows them up with nuclear weapons. Strange as Scientology's pseudo-theology may be, though, it's not as entertaining as the life story of the church's founder, L. Ron Hubbard.

To hear his disciples tell it, Hubbard, who died in 1986, was the subject of "universal acclaim" and one of the greatest men who ever lived. Not only did he devise the church's founding theory of Dianetics, which promises to free mankind of psychological trauma, he was a source of wisdom about everything from jazz music to nuclear physics. The official Web site dedicated to his life features subsites that expound upon his brilliant callings: "The Humanitarian," "The Philosopher," "The Writer," "The Artist," "The Poet/Lyricist," "The Music Maker," "The Yachtsman," and "Adventurer/Explorer: Daring Deeds and Unknown Realms." Visitors can hear an audio recording of Hubbard singing one of his own poems or learn about the soundtrack he composed for his 1,000-page sci-fi epic *Battlefield Earth* (later brought to Hollywood by Scientologist

John Travolta). Hubbard's composition "utilized elements from several genres—from honky-tonk and free-swinging jazz to cutting-edge electronic rock. The result is a wholly new dimension in space opera sound." (Sign me up for a copy!)

There's a deep chasm between the erudite, noble Hubbard of Scientology myth and the true identity of the church's wacky founder. To those not in his thrall, Hubbard might be better described as a pulp science-fiction writer who combined delusions of grandeur with a cynical hucksterism. Yet he turned an oddball theory about human consciousness—which originally appeared in a 25-cent sci-fi magazine—into a far-reaching and powerful multimillion-dollar empire. The church now claims to have about 8 million members in more than 100 countries. The slow creep of Scientology's anti-drug programs into public schools, the presumably tens of millions of dollars the church keeps with the help of its tax-exempt status, and the accusations that the church has convinced people to hand over their life savings make Hubbard's bizzarro legacy seem less like tragicomedy and more like a scandal. Comparable crackpots-in-chief like Lyndon LaRouche and Sun Myung Moon have had almost no detectable national influence. But famous Scientologists—Cruise, Travolta, the singer Beck, and even—say it ain't so!—the voice of Bart Simpson, have given Hubbard a veneer of popular credibility and his church a perpetual recruitment ticket.

Hubbard always imagined himself a great man of history. "All men are your slaves," he once wrote in a diary entry unearthed during a 1984 lawsuit. He reportedly once claimed to have written a manuscript that contained such brutal truths that anyone who read it went insane or committed suicide. He fancied himself a nuclear physicist, never mind his lack of training, and posited that fallout from Cold War nuclear tests was interfering with Scientology therapies. (Hubbard even wrote a book titled *All About Radiation*—a swell read, according to one reviewer on Amazon who says, "I understand radiation better and feel like I could survive an atomic explosion somewhere on the planet, if it wasn't, of course, really close to me.") He reportedly constructed the myth that he was a World War II combat hero, when in fact the Navy reprimanded him after a San Diego–based ship he commanded shelled some nearby Mexican islands for target practice.

Hubbard's version is understandably preferable to the reality, which was a dark farce. Hubbard was born in 1911 in Tilden, Neb. After flunking out of George Washington University, he became a pulp science-fiction and adventure writer. In the mid-1940s, he fell in with John Parsons, a wealthy and brilliant young rocket scientist in California, who also happened to be under the tutelage of the infamous satanist Aleister Crowley (no relation to yours truly, thankfully). According to Russell Miller's damning biography of Hubbard, *Bare-Faced Messiah*, Parsons was a science-fiction fan who briefly hosted Hubbard at his Pasadena, Calif., mansion, which featured a domed backyard temple and a rotating cast of occultists and eccentrics. Parsons described Hubbard as his "magical partner," and together the men engaged in a rite in which Parsons tried to impregnate with an antichrist child a woman he considered the whore of Babylon, a goal that Crowley had long promoted. With Rachmaninoff's "Isle of the Dead" playing in the background, Hubbard allegedly chanted spells over the copulating couple, according to Miller and others. (Ultimately Hubbard would steal Parsons' girlfriend and allegedly bilk him in a Miami yacht venture.) Years later, when Hubbard had grown famous and realized the antichrist episode didn't comport with his image as a man of culture and wisdom, he would reportedly claim to have been working on an undercover mission for U.S. Naval Intelligence to investigate black magic.

Dabbling in (or investigating) witchcraft didn't pay the bills, and by the late 1940s Hubbard was in debt and despondent. Then in 1950 he published *Dianetics: The Modern Science of Mental Health*, which he billed as "a milestone for man comparable to his discovery of fire and superior to his inventions of the wheel and arch." The theory of Dianetics promised to cure almost any physical and mental ailment—including wrinkles—by cleansing people's memories of traumatic past experiences so they could arrive at a "clear" mental state. Well poised to capitalize on a growing national fascination with psychotherapy, the book was an instant best-seller. Dianetics groups and parties sprung up nationwide.

Hubbard became an icon, and thousands of fans sought him out. In 1954, as the book's success—and his income—began to fade, Hubbard founded the Church of Scientology. His son Ron Jr. claimed in a 1983 interview with *Penthouse* that money was the motive, saying his father "told me and a lot of other people that the way to make a million was to start a religion." Hubbard made his millions quickly and used them to style himself as a sophisticated aristocrat, relocating to an English country home dubbed "Saint Hill Manor."

But Hubbard quickly alienated governments at home and abroad. He and his followers developed a reputation for intimidating critics and church defectors. An official inquiry in Australia concluded that Scientology is "evil" and "a serious threat to the community, medically, morally and socially; and its adherents sadly deluded and often medically ill." In 1963, federal agents, suspicious that Hubbard's therapy might pose a health risk, raided the church's Washington, D.C., branch. The IRS concluded soon after that Hubbard was skimming millions of dollars from church funds and revoked Scientology's tax-exempt status. (The church won back that status in 1993 after a long, fierce campaign; several European countries still don't recognize Scientology as a religion.) In 1967, Hubbard fled to the high seas for most of the next eight years. During this period he dreamed up the "Sea Org," a special branch of Scientology whose members wear sharp blue naval uniforms and sign contracts pledging their service for 1 billion years.

Hubbard finally returned to land in 1975, first to Washington, D.C., and then to the California desert. Lying low, Hubbard was doted on by a special group of teenage "messengers" who pulled on his socks and followed him with ashtrays when he smoked. He developed Howard Hughes–like eccentricities, flying into rages if he smelled detergent in his clothes, which caused the terrified messengers to rinse his laundry in multiple water buckets.

Meanwhile, the church's ongoing paranoia and vindictiveness culminated in a shockingly elaborate operation, which Hubbard dubbed "Snow White," to spy on and burglarize multiple federal offices, including the IRS and the Justice Department, with the aim of stealing and destroying government documents about Scientology. The Scientologists even planted moles in some federal offices. In 1983, 11 church leaders, including Hubbard's wife, were convicted and sentenced to prison for the conspiracy. Though Hubbard was named as a co-conspirator, he was never indicted.

By that time, in any case, he had gone into hiding. On or around Jan. 17, 1986, Hubbard suffered a catastrophic stroke on a secluded ranch near Big Sur, Calif. A week later he was dead. Scientology attorneys arrived to recover his body, which they sought to have cremated immediately. They were blocked by a county coroner, who, according to Scientology critics, did an autopsy that revealed high levels of a psychiatric drug (Vistaril). That would seem like an embarrassment given the church's hostility to such medications (witness Tom Cruise's recent feud with Brooke Shields), but it didn't stop the church from summoning thousands of followers to the Hollywood Palladium days after Hubbard's death. There they were told that Hubbard "willingly discarded the body after it was no longer useful to him," and that this signified "his ultimate success: the conquest of life that he embarked upon half a century ago." Perhaps it would be more accurate to say that Hubbard's ultimate success lay in convincing millions of people he was something other than a nut.

The Columbine Killers

At last we know why they did it.

BY DAVE CULLEN

ON APRIL 20, 1999, Eric Harris and Dylan Klebold murdered their classmates and teachers at Columbine High School. It may have been the most notorious mass murder in American history, and certainly the most notorious mass murder by children. Most Americans have reached one of two wrong conclusions about why they did it. The first conclusion is that the pair of supposed "Trench Coat Mafia outcasts" were taking revenge against the bullies who had made school miserable for them. The second conclusion is that the massacre was inexplicable: We can never understand what drove them to such horrific violence.

But the FBI and its team of psychiatrists and psychologists have reached an entirely different conclusion. They believe they know why Harris and Klebold killed, and their explanation is both more reassuring and more troubling than our misguided conclusions. Three months after the massacre, the FBI convened a summit in Leesburg, Va., that included world-renowned mental health experts, including Michigan State University psychiatrist Dr. Frank Ochberg, as well as Supervisory Special Agent Dwayne Fuselier, the FBI's lead Columbine investigator and a clinical psychologist. Fuselier and Ochberg share their conclusions publicly here for the first time.

The first steps to understanding Columbine, they say, are to forget the popular narrative about the jocks, Goths, and Trench-coat Mafia and to abandon the core idea that Columbine was simply a school shooting. We can't understand why they did it until we understand what they were doing.

School shooters tend to act impulsively and attack the targets of their rage: students and faculty. But Harris and Klebold planned for a year and dreamed much bigger. The school served as means to a grander end, to terrorize the entire nation by attacking a symbol of American life—not unlike the 9/11 hijackers aimed at the most visible symbols of American capitalism, democracy, and military power. Their slaughter was aimed at students and teachers, but it was not motivated by resentment of them in particular. Students and teachers were just convenient quarry, what Timothy McVeigh described as "collateral damage."

The killers, in fact, laughed at petty school shooters. They bragged about dwarfing the carnage of the Oklahoma City bombing and originally scheduled their bloody performance for its anniversary. Klebold boasted on video about inflicting "the most deaths in U.S. history." Columbine was intended not primarily as a shooting at all, but as a bombing on a massive scale. If they hadn't been so bad at wiring the timers, the propane bombs they set in the cafeteria would have wiped out 600 people. After those bombs went off, they planned to gun down fleeing survivors. An explosive third act would follow, when their cars, packed with still more bombs, would rip through still more crowds, presumably of survivors, rescue workers, and reporters. The climax would be captured on live television. It wasn't just "fame" they were after—Agent Fuselier bristles at that trivializing term—they were gunning for devastating infamy on the historical scale of an Attila the Hun. Their vision was to create a nightmare so devastating and apocalyptic that the entire world would shudder at their power.

Harris and Klebold would have been dismayed that Columbine was dubbed the "worst school shooting in American history." They set their sights on eclipsing the world's greatest mass murderers, but the media never saw past the choice of venue. The school setting drove analysis in precisely the wrong direction.

Fuselier and Ochberg say that if you want to understand "the killers," quit asking what drove them. Eric Harris and Dylan Klebold were radically different individuals, with vastly different motives and opposite mental conditions. Klebold is easier to comprehend, a more familiar type. He was hotheaded, but depressive and suicidal. He blamed himself for his problems.

Harris is the challenge. He was sweet-faced and well-spoken. Adults, and even some other kids, described him as "nice." But Harris was cold, calculating, and homicidal. "Klebold was hurting inside while Harris wanted to hurt people," Fuselier says. Harris was not merely a troubled kid, the psychiatrists say, he was a psychopath.

In popular usage, almost any crazy killer is a "psychopath." But in psychiatry, it's a very specific mental condition that rarely involves killing, or even psychosis. "Psychopaths are not disoriented or out of touch with reality, nor do they experience the delusions, hallucinations, or intense subjective distress that characterize most other mental disorders," writes Dr. Robert Hare, in *Without Conscience*, the seminal book on the condition. (Hare is also one of the psychologists consulted by the FBI about Columbine and by *Slate* for this story.) "Unlike psychotic individuals, psychopaths are rational and aware of what they are doing and why. Their behavior is the result of choice, freely exercised." Diagnosing Harris as a psychopath represents neither a legal defense nor a moral excuse. But it illuminates a great deal about the thought process that drove him to mass murder.

Diagnosing him as a psychopath was not a simple matter. Harris opened his private journal with the sentence, "I hate the f–ing world." And when the media studied Harris, they focused on his hatred—hatred that supposedly led him to revenge. It's easy to get lost in the hate, which screamed out relentlessly from Harris' Web site:

"YOU KNOW WHAT I HATE!!!? Cuuuuuuuuhntryyyyyyyyy music!!! . . .

"YOU KNOW WHAT I HATE!!!? People who say that wrestling is real!! . . .

*"YOU KNOW WHAT I HATE!!!? People who use the same word over and over again! . . . Read a f–in book or two, increase your vo-cab-u-lary f*ck*ng idiots."*

"YOU KNOW WHAT I HATE!!!? STUPID PEOPLE!!! Why must so many people be so stupid!!? . . . YOU KNOW WHAT I HATE!!!? When people mispronounce words! and they dont even know it to, like acrosT, or eXspreso, pacific (specific), or 2 pAck. learn to speak correctly you morons.

YOU KNOW WHAT I HATE!!!? STAR WARS FANS!!! GET A FaaaaaaRIGIN LIFE YOU BORING GEEEEEKS!"

It rages on for page after page and is repeated in his journal and in the videos he and Klebold made. But Fuselier recognized a far more revealing emotion bursting through, both fueling and overshadowing the hate. What the boy was really expressing was contempt.

He is disgusted with the morons around him. These are not the rantings of an angry young man, picked on by jocks until he's not going to take it anymore. These are the rantings of someone with a messianic-grade superiority complex, out to punish the entire human race for its appalling inferiority. It may look like hate, but "It's more about demeaning other people," says Hare.

A second confirmation of the diagnosis was Harris' perpetual deceitfulness. "I lie a lot," Eric wrote to his journal. "Almost constantly, and to everybody, just to keep my own ass out of the water. Let's see, what are some of the big lies I told? Yeah I stopped smoking. For doing it, not for getting caught. No I haven't been making more bombs. No I wouldn't do that. And countless other ones."

Harris claimed to lie to protect himself, but that appears to be something of a lie as well. He lied for pleasure, Fuselier says.

"Duping delight"—psychologist Paul Ekman's term—represents a key characteristic of the psychopathic profile.

Harris married his deceitfulness with a total lack of remorse or empathy—another distinctive quality of the psychopath. Fuselier was finally convinced of his diagnosis when he read Harris' response to being punished after being caught breaking into a van. Klebold and Harris had avoided prosecution for the robbery by participating in a "diversion program" that involved counseling and community service. Both killers feigned regret to obtain an early release, but Harris had relished the opportunity to perform. He wrote an ingratiating letter to his victim offering empathy rather than just apologies. Fuselier remembers that it was packed with statements like "Jeez, I understand now how you feel" and "I understand what this did to you."

"But he wrote that strictly for effect," Fuselier said. "That was complete manipulation. At almost the exact same time, he wrote down his real feelings in his journal: 'Isn't America supposed to be the land of the free? How come, if I'm free, I can't deprive a stupid f–ing dumbshit from his possessions if he leaves them sitting in the front seat of his f–ing van out in plain sight and in the middle of f–ing nowhere on a Frif–ingday night. NATURAL SELECTION. F–er should be shot.' "

Harris' pattern of grandiosity, glibness, contempt, lack of empathy, and superiority read like the bullet points on Hare's Psychopathy Checklist and convinced Fuselier and the other leading psychiatrists close to the case that Harris was a psychopath.

It begins to explain Harris' unbelievably callous behavior: his ability to shoot his classmates, then stop to taunt them while they writhed in pain, then finish them off. Because psychopaths are guided by such a different thought process than non-psychopathic humans, we tend to find their behavior inexplicable. But they're actually much easier to predict than the rest of us once you understand them. Psychopaths follow much stricter behavior patterns than the rest of us because they are unfettered by conscience, living solely for their own aggrandizement. (The difference is so striking that Fuselier trains hostage negotiators to identify psychopaths during a standoff and immediately reverse tactics if they think they're facing one. It's like flipping a switch between two alternate brain-mechanisms.)

None of his victims means anything to the psychopath. He recognizes other people only as means to obtain what he desires. Not only does he feel no guilt for destroying their lives, he doesn't grasp what they feel. The truly hard-core psychopath doesn't quite comprehend emotions like love or hate or fear, because he has never experienced them directly.

"Because of their inability to appreciate the feelings of others, some psychopaths are capable of behavior that normal people find not only horrific but baffling," Hare writes. "For example, they can torture and mutilate their victims with about the same sense of concern that we feel when we carve a turkey for Thanksgiving dinner."

The diagnosis transformed their understanding of the partnership. Despite earlier reports about Harris and Klebold being equal partners, the psychiatrists now believe firmly that Harris was the mastermind and driving force. The partnership did enable Harris to stray from typical psychopathic behavior in one way. He restrained himself. Usually psychopathic killers crave the stimulation of violence. That is why they are often serial killers—murdering regularly to feed their addiction. But Harris managed to stay (mostly) out of trouble for the year that he and Klebold planned the attack. Ochberg theorizes that the two killers complemented each other. Cool, calculating Harris calmed down Klebold when he got hot-tempered. At the same time, Klebold's fits of rage served as the stimulation Harris needed.

The psychiatrists can't help speculating what might have happened if Columbine had never happened. Klebold, they agree, would never have pulled off Columbine without Harris. He might have gotten caught for some petty crime, gotten help in the process, and conceivably could have gone on to live a normal life.

Their view of Harris is more reassuring, in a certain way. Harris was not a wayward boy who could have been rescued. Harris, they believe, was irretrievable. He was a brilliant killer without a conscience, searching for the most diabolical scheme imaginable. If he had lived to adulthood and developed his murderous skills for many more years, there is no telling what he could have done. His death at Columbine may have stopped him from doing something even worse.

Baseball

Why it's always dying.

BY JOSH LEVIN

THE MIDDLE 2000S HAVE BEEN a fruitful era for baseball's apocalypse watchers. In his book *Juiced*, Jose Canseco described the masterful technique he used to inject steroids into Mark McGwire's ample posterior. Canseco, McGwire, Sammy Sosa, and Rafael Palmeiro were frogmarched in front of Congress to explain their musclebound physiques. Dogged reporters from the *San Francisco Chronicle* implicated the record-setting Barry Bonds in the game's roids scandal, too. "I hate it. I don't want to believe any of it. . . . But this steroid stuff is ruining everything," wrote the *Boston Globe's* Dan Shaughnessy in 2004. Beware, baseball fans, the end is nigh!

Even if the drugs scandal melts away this summer, or next summer, you can be sure that the game will be perched on death's door again soon. Loving baseball is hating what it has become, then falling in love all over again. No other American sport or institution is caught in such a cycle of death and rebirth.

For more than a century, baseball reigned as the unchallenged national pastime. That the game is still ritually mourned in the age of Monday Night Football and Allen Iverson is the best evidence it still matters. As Ken Burns would (comprehensively) tell you, the game's historical and cultural impact has been immense. Troops tossed the horsehide across enemy lines during the Civil War; Japanese soldiers cursed Babe Ruth to American GIs during

World War II; Jackie Robinson's 1947 major league debut was a watershed moment for the sport and the nation.

All those years of cultural supremacy gave the grand old game a nice running start on screwing up. Countless evil forces, from the destruction of Ebbets Field to the high mound to artificial turf to free agency to interleague play to contraction, have threatened to wipe the scourge of baseball from the planet. And since baseball is the sepia-toned game of Little League, *Field of Dreams*, and a catch with dad, each time it happens, we weep that we're losing our national innocence all over again.

So, how does baseball manage to keep performing its Lazarus act? The courts save it, a charismatic player saves it, our willful ignorance saves it, an unquenchable need for our men in uniform saves it. The major leagues faced the guillotine during their formative years when, in 1914, the Federal League tried to go big-time. The upstart league's hefty paychecks wooed Hall of Famers like Chief Bender and Three Finger Brown from their American and National League franchises. Rather than pay the new market value for his players, Connie Mack dismantled his AL champion Philadelphia A's. The A's went directly from the World Series to a 43–109 record.

AL and NL owners fought back in the courtroom, repeatedly suing Federal League owners for prying away top talent. The FL countersued, arguing that the teams of organized baseball constituted a monopoly. The case landed before the reliably trust-busting Judge Kenesaw Mountain Landis. This time, Landis let the majors keep their monopoly, and the debt-laden FL ultimately settled out of court in 1915. FL owners got $600,000, the major leagues absorbed two FL teams, and the FL disbanded. The lesson, as decreed by the Supreme Court a few years later: Baseball is no mere business, but a sacred trust.

With everything right in baseball land, Landis was rewarded for his judicial indecisiveness with his appointment as MLB's first commissioner. He presided over the game's next brush with death, the Black Sox scandal. Eight members of the Chicago White Sox, including lifetime .356 hitter Shoeless Joe Jackson, were banned from the game for conspiring to fix the 1919 World Series. As tear-soaked, floppy-hatted newsboys moaned, "Say it ain't so, Joe," Babe Ruth blotted their eyes, reviving interest in the game with his offensive prowess. In 1920, Ruth walloped 54 home runs, a ridiculous 25 more than the record he had set the year prior. In 1921, the year the Black Sox went on trial, Ruth again broke the record with 59 long balls.

Though strikes and lockouts had become a matter of course by the 1970s, the 1994–1995 strike caused what none of baseball's other near-death experiences (at least those that took place after 1904) could manage: the cancellation of the World Series. It also inspired historic levels of venomous spew directed at the game's greedy players and owners. With squads of replacement players ready to trot out on Opening Day, angry fans and newspaper columnists vowed to boycott the game forever. The sides settled before any replacement games were played, and forever ended a few weeks later. Cal Ripken's proletarian pursuit of Lou Gehrig's consecutive-games streak offered a parallel force for good. Attendance still lagged behind pre-strike levels, though, and the public's imagination wasn't truly recaptured until the touchy-feely, andro-fueled McGwire-Sosa home-run chase of 1998.

Baseball fathers pass to their children not just a misty-eyed nostalgia, but also a series of sacred numbers: 60, 61, 70, and 73; 714 and 755. These, too, are a source of mourning. Each time the game's records are surpassed, there's rejoicing, then recoiling, then a hunt for a scapegoat. No matter that every player's stats are tainted by something: endemic racism, the live ball, the dead ball, the spitball, World War II, the Korean War, small ballparks, the DH, the dilution of pitching—the latest taint is always the most tainted of them all. When Roger Maris hit 61 in '61, Commissioner Ford Frick pleaded for an asterisk on account of the 162-game season. When Mark McGwire and then Barry Bonds surpassed Maris' mark by bloating their bodies like cartoon characters, we cheered the gentle giants, then chided them in hindsight for their artificially induced gigantism.

Drug use is the modern age's most reliable destroyer of sandlot innocence. Jim Bouton's 1970 book *Ball Four*, with its wild and wooly tales of clubhouse amphetamine use, shocked fans and Commissioner Bowie Kuhn. The so-called Pittsburgh cocaine trials in 1985 proved even seamier. As part of the case against Philadelphia Phillies caterer Curtis Strong, seven major leaguers admitted their coke habits in open court in exchange for immunity. Keith Hernandez estimated that up to 250 players snorted what he called "the devil on this earth"; Pittsburgh's mascot, the Pirate Parrot, was implicated for helping players acquire cocaine. The players who testified avoided suspension by tithing their salaries to antidrug charities. Commissioner Peter Ueberroth was generally lauded for cracking down on drugs. "I believe baseball is going to be the first sport to be free of drugs. The players have had enough of it," he said.

While baseball dies a new death every time it shows human frailty—money-grubbing, drug-taking, lying, cheating—moralizing partisans show their human sides too, perpetually forgiving America's prodigal game for its latest transgression. The columnists and fans who finally had their illusions crushed by this winter's scandal will be back in their seats by Opening Day, just in time to be crushed by the next one. Since there's no Babe Ruth—not even a Babe Ruth on steroids—to save the game this year, perhaps we should look to Steve Howe as our baseball totem. Howe is the former Dodgers and Yankees reliever who was suspended for drug use seven times before finally being banned for life in 1992. A few months later, he was reinstated. An arbitrator said the penalty was too harsh.

Jesus Christ

Choose your own savior.

BY CHRIS SUELLENTROP

WHEN MEL GIBSON RESPONDED to critics of his blockbuster *The Passion of the Christ* by saying they had a "problem with the four Gospels," not with his film, he was staking a claim to authenticity: My Jesus is the real one, not yours.

But it's not just Mel. Everyone claims their Jesus is the "real" one, the only authentic Christ unperverted by secular society or religious institutions. The best-selling novel *The Da Vinci Code*, which posits among other things that Jesus fathered a child by Mary Magdalene, styles itself as a fact-based account of the "real" Jesus, who has been covered up by a Vatican conspiracy. Academics who seek evidence for the Jesus of history attempt to peel away layers of the Gospel narratives until the genuine Jewish prophet is revealed—or draw on newly discovered ancient texts, such at the Gospel of Judas, to explain him. Nowadays, even nonbelievers assert a superior understanding of who the actual Jesus really was and what he stood for.

Why can everyone from atheists to Zoroastrians lay claim to knowledge of the real Jesus? Because there are so many of him. The New Testament itself presents multiple Jesuses, not just among the four competing Gospel accounts but within each Gospel as well: Baby Jesus, Teacher Jesus, Miracle Worker Jesus, to name only three. Over the course of an Easter weekend, Christians will move from honoring one Jesus, the suffering and dying

Jesus of Good Friday, to revering another one, the Risen Lord of Easter Sunday. The old theological conundrum has a new twist: How many Jesuses can dance on the head of a pin?

The most popular Jesus of the moment may be the Manly Messiah, a macho savior unbowed by pain or torment. The logo of the Lord's Gym franchises may be the best example: A ripped, muscular Jesus does push-ups while carrying a cross emblazoned with the phrase "the sins of the world" across his back. You get the feeling that bearing the cross is akin to a soldier dropping and giving 20—it's unpleasant but not all that burdensome. This Jesus wouldn't fall three times on the road to Golgotha, and he certainly wouldn't need Simon of Cyrene to help carry the cross.

The Manly Messiah is a man of action, not wordy parables, so the New Testament incident of choice for his partisans is the overturning of the moneychangers' tables in the Temple. A close cousin of the Manly Messiah is the Apocalyptic Jesus of Revelation, what the *New York Times* has called the "Warrior Jesus."

In *The Passion*, Gibson creates still another manly Jesus. By merging the suffering, human Jesus of the Stations of the Cross with a more macho conception of Christ, he's given birth to Rocky Jesus.

Rocky Jesus displays his manliness by enduring unimaginable pain. After taking a fist in the eye early in the film, James Caviezel spends the next two hours looking very much like the Italian Stallion at the end of his bruising matches with Apollo Creed. (Rocky Jesus differs markedly from another boxing Jesus, the unblemished champion Jesus of the painting *Undefeated*.) Later, after being brutally lashed during the scourging, Gibson's Jesus gathers his strength, pulls himself off the floor, and stands, defiant. He's quickly thrashed into submission again, but the message is clear: Jesus is beaten but not broken. He went the distance. Yo, Mary, I did it.

In his book *American Jesus*, Stephen Prothero shows how early 20th-century proponents of a masculine Jesus were reacting to the feminine, *Queer Eye for the Christ Guy* portraits of Jesus that were popular in the 19th century. Prothero points to the absurdly womanish, wide-hipped Jesus of *El Señor, Andando Sobre el Mar* (*Christ Walking on the Sea*) as perhaps the best example. In the 21st century, feminine Jesus lives on as the ultimate sensitive man. South Park mocks this Jesus: Its Christ hosts a Donahue-style talk show called *Jesus and Pals*.

This is Blue-State Jesus, a pacifist Democrat who drives a hybrid vehicle while advising people to cheerfully render their taxes unto Caesar. Blue-State Jesus is an anti-authoritarian hippie who judges not lest he be judged. ("Following a set of rules doesn't make us the Father's children," grooved one 1960s San Francisco Bay Area group cited by Prothero. "It's digging on the relationship with Him.") A few years back, People for the Ethical Treatment of Animals launched a Blue-State Jesus campaign when they tried to convince Americans that the Lamb of God didn't eat meat. Blue-State Jesus might be black or gay. He dislikes organized religion. He's more economic radical than sexual conservative. Sure, he opposed divorce and adultery, but didn't he save an adulteress from a stoning? Blue-State Jesus was the driving force behind abolitionism and the civil rights movement but not the pro-life or temperance movements. Heck, he's Party Jesus—he turns water into wine just to keep the night rockin'.

Which of these Jesuses—and the countless others that exist—is the real Jesus? In a sense, they all are. The emergence of Jesus as a computer programmer in *The Matrix* shows how he can be reinvented for any age, even the future. But in another sense, none of them is the real Jesus. He remains a mystery.

Scholars have sought out the Historical Jesus in an effort to solve the riddle. The consensus is that he was a Jew who lived between 4 B.C. and A.D. 30, that he thought the end of the world was at hand, that he was considered a healer and miracle worker ("of a sort well known in Judaism," E.P. Sanders wrote in the *New York Review of Books*), that he used parables to teach about God and ethics, that Pontius Pilate ordered him crucified, and that his followers believed he rose from the dead. But historians can't answer the most pressing question: Was he the Son of God?

The Historical Jesus wasn't the Jesus who inspired Paul, the salesman of the new religion of Christianity, who never met Jesus of Nazareth. On the road to Damascus, Paul encountered the risen Jesus, the so-called Living Jesus, the Christ of faith. That's the Jesus that most Christians seek to know and to understand.

TYRANTS

Kim Jong-il

North Korea's international man of mystery.

BY CHRIS SUELLENTROP

SINCE THE COLLAPSE of the Soviet Union, Pyongyangology has replaced Kremlinology as the favored sport of Communist-watchers. It's a tricky exercise: Few know what really goes on inside North Korea, much less what motivates the nation's perplexing leader, Kim Jong-il. As a result, most North Korean analysts have a predictive record that falls somewhere between poor and abysmal.

A quick scorecard: In 1994, when Kim Jong-il formally took power after the death of his father, Kim Il Sung, most experts foresaw the almost immediate collapse of the son's regime. Kim Jr. was thought to be a drunken lech, too busy partying and chasing tail to survive long. But he kept a firm grip on power despite ruinous floods and a famine that killed upwards of 2 million of his subjects. Then, when Kim met with South Korea's Kim Dae-jung for a historic summit in June 2000, his image underwent a revision. The new Kim was rumored to be the totalitarian version of George W. Bush, a pampered political son who, after a misspent youth, developed into a capable leader. In 2002, after North Korea acknowledged that it's been developing nuclear weapons despite promises not to do so, Kim's reputation was revised once again: North Korea's international man of mystery is more Dr. Evil than Austin Powers.

Which isn't to say that he doesn't have a little Austin in him. After all, Kim is a short, anachronistic party animal who boasts a silly haircut, elevated shoes, and goofy glasses, and who almost always wears the same outfit. Although Kim's dissolute exploits have likely been exaggerated by South Korean intelligence, he's still thought to be a heavy drinker with a fondness for blondes. (Perhaps he was actually referring to his taste in women when he told Secretary of State Madeleine Albright in 2000 that, economically, he was intrigued by "the Swedish model.")

But Kim is a more serious leader than many first thought. He's been running much of the North Korean government for decades. According to Kongdan Oh and Ralph C. Hassig's *North Korea: Through the Looking Glass*, Kim's father picked Kim Jong-il to succeed him in the early '70s, after which the son slowly took control of the levers of power. He preferred to work behind the scenes, and in a sense he still does: Even in death, dear old Dad holds the titular position of "eternal president." (Think of Kim Il Sung as the dictator-for-afterlife.)

Like many sons, Kim didn't always want to follow in his father's footsteps. What he really wants to do is direct. Kim's video library reputedly contains between 15,000 and 20,000 films, and in 1973 he wrote a 300-page book on film, titled *On the Subject of the Cinema*. In a less academic vein, he authorized the separate kidnappings of a South Korean movie director and his wife in 1978. After keeping them apart for five years (with neither knowing of the other's whereabouts), Kim reunited them and explained that he hoped to turn North Korea into some kind of East Asian Hollywood with their help. The three made six movies together before the two captives escaped, including one that won a best-director award at a Czechoslovakian film festival. In a 1994 interview with the *Los Angeles Times*, the liberated actress-wife said Kim could have been a top-notch movie producer had fate not led him down the path of totalitarian dictatorship. "We nicknamed him 'micro-manager,'" she said. "He pays attention to everything. He keeps track of everything. He is simply amazing."

When Mr. Micromanager isn't on the set, however, his temper can get the best of him. His fingerprints are thought to be on a 1983 bombing that offed most of the South Korean Cabinet. He's also thought to have given the order to blow up a South Korean passenger plane in 1987, killing 115 passengers. The motive? Kim wanted to keep people away from Seoul's 1988 Olympics. The evils Kim has visited on his own country are even more horrifying—Stalinist gulags, secret police, and a populace that starves while Kim spends $900 million on dad's mausoleum. According to Anne Applebaum, visitors to Pyongyang report that starving women can be seen "surreptitiously eating grass in the city parks."

It would be easy to dismiss Kim as a madman, but his behavior is too consistent for that. The trick North Korea pulled on the United States over the two countries' nuclear weapons agreement is a familiar one. As Asia analyst Chuck Downs has outlined, North Korea's negotiating behavior is predictable. First, North Korea "agrees in principle" to a deal; later, the North "reinterprets" the agreement; and finally, it blames its negotiating partner for "the failure of talks."

Kim has used these tactics in almost every one of his recent diplomatic efforts. The Korean peace process hasn't gone very far: Since the historic Kim-Kim summit, Kim Jong-il has reneged on a number of agreements, particularly embarrassing Kim Dae-jung by not setting a date for a promised trip to Seoul. Kim turned to the same page of his negotiating handbook when dealing with Russia: Vladimir Putin thought he reached a deal with Kim to stop North Korea's development of missiles, but Kim later said that his remarks to Putin were a "passing, laughing matter" that the Russian president had taken too seriously. And for a long time, North Korea has attributed its failure to comply with its nuclear agreements to Washington's "hostile policy" toward it.

So, perhaps Dr. Evil isn't the right Mike Myers character to describe Kim Jong-il after all. He isn't a lunatic supervillain. He's just a fat bastard.

Rupert Murdoch

He's not as bad as he seems—really.

BY DAVID PLOTZ

IT IS A TRUTH universally acknowledged that Rupert Murdoch is scum. The media tycoon has built his global empire on schlock and sleaze, used heavy-handed tactics and legal chicanery to evade laws and taxes, toppled British and Australian governments to expand his domain, all but bribed Newt Gingrich and Margaret Thatcher with sweetheart book deals, made mockery of the grand traditions of Australian/British/American journalism. His children flee the country rather than work for him. He is perhaps the world's most sinister businessman, the Ernst Blofeld of the Information Age. Even his company's name, News Corp., has an ominous, Big Brother ring to it.

So it's no wonder that the press—at least that fraction of the press he does not own—gloats about his troubles, whether it's a family squabble over his latest marriage, a $5 billion lawsuit from a jilted business partner, or a fed-up son who can't bear his dad's bossiness.

But Murdoch, inevitably, gets a raw deal. You may not like Murdoch—it's nearly impossible to like Murdoch—but you should probably admire him. He has done more to help the great mass of media consumers than anyone in the world. Murdoch is the global capitalist par excellence, the very model of free enterprise and entrepreneurship. Almost single-handedly, Murdoch has modernized the world's media, forcing competition on stagnant businesses, cracking open monopolies and oligopolies, vanquishing "traditions" that were often an excuse for laziness, unleashing the creative destruction of capitalism on an industry that thought itself exempt from it.

Everywhere Murdoch has gone, competition, efficiency, and consumer choice (and profit) have followed. In his launching pad, Australia, Murdoch bought weak papers, outworked established rivals, and became the market leader. In Great Britain, he dragged the newspaper industry into the 20th century. In 1986 he broke the press operators' union. He won the eternal enmity of British lefties, but he was right: The unions were lazy and intransigent. By sloughing off thousands of make-work employees and ditching absurd union rules (which had banned computerization, for example), Murdoch made his newspapers cheaper for readers and more profitable for him. (Murdoch's critics rarely acknowledge that publishers all over the world—including liberal saint Katharine Graham—have crushed press unions to stay afloat.) Murdoch's British satellite-TV operation, BSkyB, shattered the BBC's near monopoly on programming. British terrestrial broadcasters had limited viewers to only a handful of channels. Murdoch's satellites gave them dozens.

In the United States, too, Murdoch has greased the wheels of capitalism. Critics savaged his tabloids—the *New York Post*, the *Boston Herald*, the *Chicago Sun-Times* (he no longer owns the latter two)—as grotesque conservative rags. Which they were. But they also grabbed market share from big complacent dailies and awakened the sleepy local news trade. Murdoch brought the same fierce energy to the self-satisfied American TV industry. He broke up a four-decade oligopoly by starting a fourth network, a feat that no one, least of all ABC, CBS, and NBC, thought possible. (At the time he bought his first seven U.S. TV stations for $2 billion, industry analysts said he'd paid too much for them. They don't say that anymore.) While Fox has certainly splashed its share of garbage on the screen (e.g., *Studs, Temptation Island, So You Think You Can Dance?*), it has also given viewers some of television's most remarkable shows (*The Simpsons, 24, The X-Files, America's Most Wanted*). His Fox News Channel is partisan and brutal, but it has dominated cable news because it's so much more entertaining and energetic than its rivals. Murdoch is also wildly smarter about new media than your average mogul, buying MySpace before it got huge and purchasing a large chunk of DirecTV.

The hatred of Murdoch is, at its core, aesthetic. Murdoch's in-your-face conservatism is alienating. His newspapers and TV shows exaggerate and distort for the sake of sensationalism. They deny the very existence of good taste and propriety.

Murdoch is immune to such criticism. He's a billionaire. He was also born in Australia, which makes him, almost by definition, disrespectful of elites. He derides the BBC and respectable newspapers as "unpopular" media subsidized by a condescending, out-of-touch gentry. ("Popular" is the highest praise in the Murdoch lexicon.) Murdoch may be a modernist in his pursuit of a global techno-empire, but he's also an anachronism, a throwback to Hearst and Pulitzer. British and American journalism used to be competitive, sensational, overtly political, and populist. Murdoch believes that the snobs have crippled the profession with respectability, making journalism irrelevant to the masses. Murdoch has done all he could to restore that scrappiness. Murdoch is, in some sense, the best democrat of all: He prints newspapers that people want to read and produces TV shows that people want to watch. His British tabloid the *Sun* has the largest circulation of any English-language newspaper in the world. Populism is popular.

Sadly, Murdoch the robber baron won't be with us forever. He's past 70, and though his latest wife is half his age, he can't keep up his hectic pace. Murdoch hopes to pass on News Corp.'s control to his occasionally estranged children. He undoubtedly hopes they inherit his prickly, fierce independence. Murdoch built his empire on resentment, on proving the status quo was wrong and lazy. But thanks to his hard work, News Corp. now is the status quo. Who is left for it to rage against?

The Dictator's Son

Odai, Qusai, and other progeny of evil.

BY FRANKLIN FOER

EVER SINCE CHARLIE CHAPLIN'S *The Great Dictator*, the modern tyrant has inhabited his own comedic archetype: the vainglorious, bumbling buffoon. And ever since, high-minded critics have damned this portrayal as a vacuous diversion from reality. But there's a figure who actually conforms to the Hollywood vision of the slapstick strongman: the dictator's son.

It was hardly surprising that U.S. forces killed Odai and Qusai Hussein on July 23, 2003, six months before capturing their father, or that the brothers picked such an obvious hiding place—a cousin's home. (Perhaps they could have survived longer if they had followed their father's lead and camped out in a spider hole.) Haplessness is an essential characteristic of the dictator's son and the root of his unwitting comic genius.

Almost all modern dictators dream of handing power over to their progeny. But aside from a few exceptions (Syria's Bashar Assad and North Korea's Kim Jong-il), dictators raise sons who abjectly fail at the family business. In Africa, the children of Jomo Kenyatta, Idi Amin, and Daniel arap Moi have all made a hash of political careers handed to them on platters. Stalin's younger son, Vasily, died a miserable drunk despite inheriting his father's goon squad of Tonton Macoutes, Baby Doc couldn't hold Haiti for a third generation of Duvaliers—after a 2004 coup removed Aristide from power, Baby Doc's offers to return to his home country

y welcome. (Even more pathetically, in French exile
d $120 million and suffered evictions from multiple
fter failing at a military career, Augusto Pinochet's
ied to exploit his father's infamy, by marketing Pinochet brand credit cards and Don Augusto wine. Then he was convicted of accepting a stolen vehicle and illegally possessing firearms in Chile. Keeping things consistent, Pinochet's younger son was arrested in France on tax evasion charges in 2005.

Their failures have nothing to do with diminished capacity for evil. As far as I can discern, no dictator has ever raised a mensch. The biggest difference between father and son is the application of violence. Where the fathers calculatingly use rape, torture, and murder to tighten their grip on power, the sons throw bratty temper tantrums. Odai Hussein was especially prone to flying off the handle. Upon learning that a servant had helped Saddam's liaison with a mistress, Odai shot the underling dead in front of foreign dignitaries. The son of former Liberian strongman Charles Taylor, Chucky, reportedly flogged his chauffeur to death after the driver accidentally hit a dog and scratched his car. Two days after his father was turned over to a war crimes tribunal in Sierra Leone, Chucky was arrested by U.S. authorities upon arrival at Miami International Airport on a charge of passport fraud.

Dictators' sons are often done in by their lifestyles. Almost to a man, they have drinking and drug problems. At a summit meeting with his South Korean counterpart, Kim Jong-il reportedly knocked back 10 glasses of wine. After swilling whiskey, Odai liked to fire automatic weapons; Baby Doc regularly consumed French champagne by the case; and Nicu Ceausescu had a fondness for Johnny Walker Black. (In his 1990 trial, Nicu tried to self-exculpate by claiming that he ordered violent crackdowns only when drunk.) Both Marko Milosevic and Chucky Taylor have been accused of turning their own fondness for white lines into profit-making ventures.

This is only the tip of their self-indulgence. Dictators' sons are often described as "womanizers" and "playboys." But these words are usually just a euphemism for vicious sexual predation. Odai was a notorious rapist and would beat his wife senseless. Nicu Ceausescu kept a special rape chamber and would collect panties as trophies. According to a former U.S. ambassador, his approach of females often entailed forcefully snatching wives from their husbands. While Nicu availed himself of the wife, his guards would beat the crap out of her husband. (The *Times* of London has reported that his victims included the gymnast Nadia Comaneci.)

These weaknesses might be surmountable if the sons devoted themselves to political machination. But most sons of dictators would rather pursue vanity projects than expend shoe leather on brutal power-wielding. Because they have the power to do whatever they want—nobody tells a dictator's son "no"—they fulfill every male's fantasy of becoming sports stars and impresarios. Marko Milosevic raced cars and Baby Doc raced motorcycles, using the palace gardens as a practice track.

But soccer is the favorite pastime of the dictator's son. Both Odai Hussein and Saadi Qaddafi spent vast time and resources personally overseeing their national teams. Their motivational techniques and management style come straight from their fathers. After Iraq lost matches, Odai reprimanded his players by caning their feet and forcing them to kick cement balls. Saadi humbly selected himself to start in the Libyan national squad's midfield. It's far from clear that he deserves the spot: One of his Italian coaches told the paper *Corriere dello Sport*, "as a footballer, he's worthless." But when he played for his Libyan club team, he often looked like Maradona. That's because his opponents usually positioned themselves as far as possible from him on the pitch; referees gifted his club all sorts of absurd calls. And Libyans learned the hard way not to protest any of this. In 1996, after fans booed the biased refereeing, Saadi's bodyguards responded by spraying the stands with gunfire. At the same time Saadi pursued his playing career, he invested millions in glamorous European soccer clubs. Saadi then decided it wasn't enough to own a stake in the Italian teams, so he started playing for Italian clubs. Disconcertingly, he once tested positive for norandrosterone, a banned steroid. Roid rage is the last thing the son of a dictator needs.

Why do these sons turn out so badly? It will probably not surprise you to learn that dictators make bad dads. The strongman parenting style veers wildly from abuse to neglect. Stalin would blow cigarette smoke in his son Vasily's face. When Vasily's teacher sent Papa Joe a letter informing him that his son had composed a suicidal note, it took the tyrant 33 months to reply. And most devastatingly, Stalin refused a proposed prisoner swap that would release his son Yakov from a German POW camp. He quipped, "There are no prisoners of war; there are traitors." Yakov died in captivity.

If dictators were truly serious about keeping power in their family, they would forget about their sons and focus on their daughters. There's a long tradition of girls becoming successful heads of state. For a time, Indonesia was ruled by President-for-Life Sukarno's daughter Megawati Sukarnoputri, though she lost a re-election bid. Benazir Bhutto has followed her authoritarian father in and out of the Pakistani presidency. Bangladeshi politics has been similarly dominated by the daughters of strongmen. There's an important difference between these fathers and their daughters. The daughters are less inclined to torture, more prone to compromise, more liberal. Take it away, Carol Gilligan.

IMAGINARY FRIENDS

The Simpsons

Who turned America's best TV show into a cartoon?

BY CHRIS SUELLENTROP

SIMPSONS CREATOR MATT GROENING once proclaimed that a big-screen version of the long-running cartoon would either "kill the show or completely reinvigorate it." After a decade and a half of fits and starts, Homer and Marge's long-rumored big-screen debut will finally come in 2007. The movie certainly won't kill *The Simpsons*. What more damage could be done to a franchise that's already been dead for years?

At some point during its 17-season run, *The Simpsons* turned into one of the best sitcoms on television—and that's not a compliment. In the early-to-mid 1990s, to call *The Simpsons* the best show on Fox would have been a vast understatement; to say it was the best sitcom on television would have been inadequate; and to describe it as the greatest TV show in history would (and still does) minimize its importance by limiting its cultural impact to the small screen. Who knows when it happened—maybe it was when Homer visited the leprechaun jockeys in Season 11, or when he was raped by a panda in Season 12—but watching *The Simpsons* chase *Ozzie & Harriet*'s record for the longest-running sitcom (435 episodes) has been like watching the late-career Pete Rose: There's still greatness there, and you get to see a home run now and then, but mostly it's a halo of reflected glory.

The hype surrounding *The Simpsons'* 300th episode in 2003 underscored the show's decline. To celebrate the milestone, *Entertainment Weekly* picked the top 25 episodes in *Simpsons* history: Twenty-four of them came from 1997 or before. Similarly, *USA Today* published a top-10 list written by the fan who runs the best *Simpsons* site on the Web. He picked nine shows from 1993 and before, and the other was from 1997. The newspaper also asked *Simpsons* staff members to select their 15 favorite moments and episodes, and only one person (Al Jean, the show's executive producer) chose something that happened since 1998. Even as fans, critics, and staff members rejoice in the show's amazing longevity and its passage to the silver screen, they all agree: The past seven or eight seasons just haven't been up to snuff.

Who's to blame for this state of events? Some of the die-hard fans who populate the news group alt.tv.simpsons have settled on a "lone gunman" theory—that one man single-handedly brought down TV's Camelot. One problem: They don't agree on who's hiding in the book depository. Many fans finger Mike Scully, who served as executive producer for Seasons 9 through 12 (generally considered the show's nadir). Others target writer Ian Maxtone-Graham. Scully and Maxtone-Graham, both of whom joined the show after it had already been on the air for several seasons, are cited as evidence that *The Simpsons* lost touch with what made it popular in the beginning—Matt Groening's and James L. Brooks' conception of an animated TV family that was more realistic than the live-action Huxtables and Keatons and Seavers who populated 1980s television. Unlike other TV families, for example, the Simpsons would go to church, have money problems, and watch television.

But under Scully's tenure, *The Simpsons* became, well, a cartoon. In A.O. Scott's *Slate* "Assessment" of Matt Groening, he wrote that Groening is "committed to using cartoons as a way of addressing reality." But in recent years, *The Simpsons* has become an inversion of this. The show now uses reality as a way of addressing itself, a cartoon. One recent episode featured funny references to *Spongebob Squarepants*, the WNBA, Ken Burns, Tony Soprano, and Fox programming. But the Simpsons themselves, and the rest of the Springfield populace, have become empty vessels for one-liners and sight gags, just like the characters who inhabit other sitcoms.

The Simpsons no longer marks the elevation of the sitcom formula to its highest form. These days it's closer to *It's Garry Shandling's Show*—a very good, self-conscious parody of a sitcom (and itself). Episodes that once would have ended with Homer and Marge bicycling into the sunset (perhaps while Bart gagged in the background) now end with Homer blowing a tranquilizer dart into Marge's neck. The show's still funny, but it hasn't been touching in years. Writer Mike Reiss admitted as much to the *New York Times Magazine*, conceding that "much of the humanity has leached out of the show over the years. . . . It hurts to watch it, even if I helped do it."

But can you blame one person for it? It would be nice to finger Maxtone-Graham, who gave a jaw-dropping interview to London's *Independent* in 1998. In it, he admitted to hardly ever watching *The Simpsons* before he joined the staff in 1995, to brazenly flouting Groening's rules for the show (including saying he "loved" an episode that Groening had his name removed from), and to having open disdain for fans, saying, "Go figure! That's why they're on the Internet and we're writing the show." But just because Maxtone-Graham is a jerk (or at the very least, shows colossally bad judgment in front of an interviewer) doesn't mean he's a bad writer. On top of that, a show like *The Simpsons* is the product of so many creative individuals that it's difficult to blame one person—even Scully, the onetime executive producer—for anything.

So, instead, there are a few conspiracy theories for the show's not-quite demise. Perhaps the problem is too many cooks, as staff legend George Meyer implied to MSNBC.com: "We have more writers now," Meyer said. "In the early days, I think, more of the show, more of the episode was already in the first draft of the script. Now there's more room-writing that goes on, and so I think there's been a kind of homogenization of the scripts. . . . Certainly, the shows are more jokey than they used to be. But I think they also lack the individual flavor that they had in the early years." Another theory lays the blame on the show's many celebrity guest stars, which have made the show resemble those old *Scooby Doo* episodes where Sandy Duncan, or Tim Conway and Don Knotts, would show up just for the heck of it. Still others think the problem is the show's brain drain: Long-absent individuals include creators Groening and Brooks, actor Phil Hartman, and writers Al Jean and Mike Reiss (who both left briefly to do *The Critic*), Greg Daniels (who left to do *King of the Hill*), and Conan O'Brien (who has been linked to the show's decline so many times that Groening once called the theory "one of the most annoying nut posts" on the Internet).

But maybe no one, not even a group of people, can be held responsible. *Simpsons* determinists lay the blame on unstoppable, abstract forces like time. The show's writers and producers often subscribe to this line when they publicly abase themselves for not living up to the show's high standards. Maxtone-Graham told the *Independent*, "I think we should pack it in soon and I think we will—we're running out of ideas," and Meyer admitted to MSNBC.com, "We're starting to see some glimmers of the end. . . . It's certainly getting harder to come up with stories, no question."

An incredible anxiety of influence hovers over *Simpsons* writers, who realize that they are judged not by the standards of network television, but by the standards of their own show's golden age. By the end of his tenure as executive producer, Scully was making nervous statements to the press like, "Basically, my goal is just not to wreck the show." In an interview about the movie, Al Jean sounds consumed by fear: "If I were feeling any more pressure, I'd be a diamond."

Maybe *The Simpsons* is killing *The Simpsons* by setting expectations too high. After all, even while you're wincing or groaning at a particularly lame gag, you're hoping that the show will stay on the air longer than Gunsmoke. It's hard to imagine television without *The Simpsons*. If it sticks around for another 400 episodes or another dozen feature films, maybe, someday, the wounds of the past decade will be remembered like the one Maggie administered to Mr. Burns: an accident, and not a fatal one.

Man of the Year

An extraordinary life.

BY DAVID PLOTZ

A VISIONARY HAS THE POWER to imagine what the world can be, and a revolutionary has the power to make it so. Very few men are either. Our Man of the Year is both. Ideas have consequences, and it is this year that we have seen the consequences of his. With his pinwheeling, hopscotch creativity, he has changed the nation's center of gravity, reinventing commerce, art, science, technology, and faith. His animating spirit—a pragmatic, idealistic humanitarianism—is rapidly becoming the ethos of the age. His passing comments roil financial markets from Bangkok to Bond Street. Hollywood moguls make pilgrimages to his seaside home. Bill Gates seeks his counsel. So does Dick Cheney. Nelson Mandela is godfather to his children. He is, it is said, the only man who plays golf with Bill Clinton and doesn't let him cheat.

Still, he is not yet a household name and may not be for some time. He is an unassuming man—a thatch of sandy hair, a pair of inquisitive brown eyes, a slight shadow of beard at all hours of the day. In a year of spectacular emotion, his was a quiet triumph. He doesn't touch the heart as Princess Diana did, the soul as Pope John Paul did, or the conscience as Bono does. But while other people make headlines, he is making history. When they chronicle our time, it should be his name that appears on the roll of honor.

But only if . . . His vision and his revolution are high-risk gambles. If they fail—and no one can predict if they will—our world will be a more dangerous place, a darker, poorer place, a world untethered from the kind of stability we have come to cherish. And if he succeeds? "Every so often God blesses us," says his close friend and confidant the Dalai Lama, "and he is such a blessing."

To understand him, to understand both his leathery toughness and his gentle soul, follow U.S. Route 44 west from Lubbock, Texas, for 50 miles. Here, 50 miles from Lubbock and 50 miles from nowhere, is a one-stoplight town called Poseyville. And here, up the block from the River Diner—though there's no river for miles—is a three-room cabin. It is in this cabin, five decades ago, that his mother came, alone, a young widow trying to start over with her 2-year-old boy. That little house was his crucible. They grew up together, mother and son. They studied together on the oilcloth-covered kitchen table, beneath the only electric light in the house. He learned his ABCs; she slowly, slowly earned her degree via correspondence. And when the lessons were over, she instilled in him the homespun wisdom that her parents had instilled in her: "The power is the word, not the sword." "There is no difficulty so great that it cannot be overcome, no triumph so great that it cannot be destroyed." His mother still lives in the same house, but electric lights are everywhere now. He phones her every day, at noon sharp. (Once he excused himself from an audience with the pope to call.)

"From the time he was a boy," she confides, "I knew that destiny had reserved him a seat." If destiny had indeed reserved him a seat, it was in the very front of the classroom. He was an A student at Poseyville High. He was also a three-sport star and "the most ferocious competitor I've ever seen," his coach says today. Even as a teen-ager, he showed signs of his independent-mindedness. His friends mowed lawns; he climbed mountains. They took piano lessons; he taught himself the trombone and busked for dimes on Main Street.

"Adversity," wrote the poet Rainer Maria Rilke, "is the seedling of courage." And adversity came. He headed east for college on scholarship. His mother, alone again, fell ill. School was a struggle. Midway through his freshman year, he gave up, hitchhiked home, and told his mother he was back for good to take care of her. That night, they went out for a walk on the plains. "It was," he says, "a clear, moonlit night. We walked by an old ranch house, and I could see the barbed wire and the old brands glinting in the moonlight. All of a sudden I thought of when the world was young and growing and full of hope. And I wanted to make it so again." The next morning, he hitchhiked back East.

His mind burns with a bright, clear flame, and his professors soon recognized his genius. He earned his degree in three years and went to work. He astonished. "He could see around corners," says an old colleague. He overturned conventional wisdom, and preached heresy. In the beginning, he was dismissed as a crackpot—at best an eccentric, at worst a threat. But steadily his fame and power and influence grew. He was not an intellectual, and he had no time for ideology, but he had the American genius for common sense. His own powerful ideas rooted themselves in society's cracks and began to sprout in all directions. And sprout. And sprout.

Today, despite his fame, he remains a startlingly humble man. Every morning, while he's in the bath, he tries to answer his dozens of personal letters. He's never missed a high-school reunion, and he still finds time to eat dinner with childhood friends twice a week. "When he got famous, I was sure he'd forget us," says one old playmate, "but he hasn't." His charm is legendary. So is his equanimity. When his aides panic over some nugget of bad news, he calms them down by quoting his sages: Lao Tzu, Euripedes, Toynbee, Covey.

Every day, he says, he receives a letter or two urging him to run for president. He laughs the idea off. The president is a captive.

He is a free man, and in freedom is true power. This is, he says, only the beginning of his crusade. In the third century, after the invention of the fulcrum and lever, Archimedes wrote, "Give me where to stand, and I will move the earth." It is now the 21st century. The Man of the Year has two feet planted squarely on the ground. And the earth is moving.

Harry Potter

Pampered jock, patsy, fraud.

BY CHRIS SUELLENTROP

LIKE MOST HEROES, Harry Potter possesses the requisite Boy Scout virtues: trustworthy, loyal, helpful, friendly, courteous, kind, obedient, cheerful, thrifty, brave, clean, and reverent. But so do lots of boys and girls, and they don't get books and movies named after them. Why isn't the book called *Ron Weasley and the Chamber of Secrets*? Why isn't its sequel dubbed *Hermione Granger and the Prisoner of Azkaban*? Why Harry? What makes him so special?

Simple: He's a glory hog who unfairly receives credit for the accomplishments of others and who skates through school by taking advantage of his inherited wealth and his establishment connections. Harry Potter is no braver than his best friend, Ron Weasley, just richer and better-connected. Harry's other good friend, Hermione Granger, is smarter and a better student. The one thing Harry excels at is the sport of Quidditch, and his pampered-jock status allows him to slide in his studies, as long as he brings the school glory on the playing field. But as Charles Barkley long ago noted, being a good athlete doesn't make you a role model.

Harry Potter is a fraud, and the cult that has risen around him is based on a lie. Potter's claim to fame, his central accomplishment in life, is surviving a curse placed on him as an infant by the evil wizard Voldemort. As a result, the wizarding world celebrates the young Harry as "The Boy Who Lived." It's a curiously passive accomplishment, akin to "The Boy Who Showed Up," or "The Boy

Who Never Took a Sick Day." And sure enough, just as none of us do anything special by slogging through yet another day, the infant Harry didn't do anything special by living. It was his mother who saved him, sacrificing her life for his.

Did your mom love you? Good, maybe you deserve to be a hero, too. The love of Harry's mother saves his life not once but twice in *Harry Potter and the Sorcerer's Stone*. Not only that, but her love for Harry sends Voldemort into hiding for 13 years, saving countless other lives in the process. The book and the movie should be named after Lily Potter. But thanks to the revisionist histories of J.K. Rowling, Lily's son is remembered as the world's savior.

What Harry has achieved on his own, without his mother, stems mostly from luck and, more often, inheritance. He's a trust-fund kid whose success at his school, Hogwarts, is largely attributable to the gifts his friends and relatives lavish upon him. A few examples: an enchanted map (made in part by his father), an invisibility cloak (his father's), and a state-of-the art magical broom (a gift from his godfather) that is the equivalent of a Lexus in a high-school parking lot. In *Harry Potter and the Half-Blood Prince*, our hero is successful primarily because he stumbles upon an old potions textbook filled with helpful marginalia—which he then uses to cheat in class.

Harry's other achievements can generally be chalked up to the fact that he regularly plays the role of someone's patsy. Almost all Harry's deeds in the first book take place under the watchful eye of Hogwarts headmaster Dumbledore, who saves Harry from certain death at the end of the book. In both *Chamber of Secrets* and *Order of the Phoenix*, the evil Voldemort successfully manipulates the unsuspecting Harry, who must once again be rescued. In *Goblet of Fire*, everything Harry accomplishes—including winning the Triwizard Tournament—takes place because he is the unwitting pawn of one of Voldemort's minions.

Even Harry's greatest moment—his climactic face-off with Voldemort in *Goblet of Fire*—isn't much to crow about. Pure happenstance is the only reason Voldemort is unable to kill Harry: Both their magic wands were made with feathers from the same bird. And even with his lucky wand, Harry still needs his mom's ghost to bail him out by telling him what to do. Once again, Lily Potter proves to be twice the man her son is.

Harry's one undisputed talent is his skill with a broom, which makes him one of the most successful Quidditch players in Hogwarts history. As Rowling puts it the first time Harry takes off on a broom, "in a rush of fierce joy he realized he'd found something he could do without being taught." Harry's talent is so natural as to be virtually involuntary. Admiring Harry for his flying skill is like admiring a cheetah for running fast. It's beautiful, but it's not an accomplishment.

In fact, Harry rarely puts hard work or effort into anything. He is a "natural." Time and again, Harry is celebrated for his instinctual gifts. When he learns that he is a Parselmouth, or someone who can speak the language of snakes, Rowling writes, "He wasn't even aware of deciding to do it." (In fact, when Harry tries to speak this language, he can't do it. He can only do it instinctively.) When Harry stabs a basilisk in *Chamber of Secrets*, Rowling writes that he did it "without thinking, without considering, as though he had meant to do it all along." In *Goblet of Fire*, during Harry's battle with Voldemort, Rowling writes that "Harry didn't understand why he was doing it, didn't know what it might achieve. . . ."

Being a wizard is something innate, something you are born to, not something you can achieve. As a result, Harry lives an effortless life. Although Dumbledore insisted, "It is our choices, Harry, that show what we truly are, far more than our abilities," the school that Dumbledore ran values native gifts above all else. That's why Harry is such a hero in wizard culture—he has the most talent, even if he hasn't done much with it. Hogwarts is nothing more than a magical Mensa meeting.

Santa Claus

Building a better Father Christmas.

BY DAVID PLOTZ

IT'S A TERRIBLE TIME to be Santa Claus. Hollywood has Father Christmas dying (*The Santa Clause*), killing (*Silent Night, Deadly Night*), robbing (*Bad Santa*), and being kidnapped (*The Nightmare Before Christmas*). Santa television ads portray him as an old lech or a clumsy oaf. American parents, who suspect all strangers, see a pedophile lurking under that bushy white beard. Some mall Santas now must keep their hands visible and touch kids only in "safe" zones. It doesn't help Kris Kringle's cause that a 71-year-old mall Santa Claus in Washington state recently pleaded guilty to raping and molesting four children between the ages of 1 and 7. The mall Santa's real name is—no joke—Ronald McDonald.

Animal-rights groups want to get rid of Santa's reindeer: Pressure from People for the Ethical Treatment of Animals forced the National Park Service to remove reindeer from their annual Mall Christmas pageant. Fundamentalist Christians want to get rid of Santa himself: He overshadows Jesus and profanes a sacred holiday. In Holland, one of St. Nick's favorite countries, he's been assaulted by teen-agers on the street and denounced by feminists. In Japan, a department store recently stumbled into the yuletide spirit by displaying Santa Claus—nailed to a crucifix. Why, mall Santas can't even say "ho ho ho" anymore: It frightens youngsters. Santa, in short, is in trouble. Any day you can expect privacy-rights advocates to start protesting at the North Pole: "Look, he sees you when you're sleeping. He knows when you're awake. He knows when you've been bad or good. And he's got a list with the name of every child in the world! Tell me that's not suspicious."

Santa needs a makeover.

It wouldn't be his first one. Santa Claus is one of America's grandest fabrications. He is, as Stephen Nissenbaum puts it in his excellent *The Battle for Christmas*, an "invented tradition." In America's early years, Christmas was a rowdy affair: Manhattan's poor and working-class folk ran wild through the streets and invaded the homes of the wealthy. So in the early 19th century, a group of rich New Yorkers took it upon themselves to domesticate Christmas. Their chief accomplishment: Clement Moore's "A Visit from St. Nicholas," the 1822 poem that introduced Americans to Santa Claus (of course you know it: "'Twas the night before Christmas . . . ").

Moore took an arcane European tradition and neatly transformed it into an American one. St. Nicholas was a real saint, a 4th-century bishop from Asia Minor famed for his generosity. The Dutch celebrated St. Nicholas on Dec. 6. On that day, he visited homes and left gifts for children by the fireplace. The Dutch St. Nicholas was an ambivalent figure: He was lean and solemn, and he gave bad children birch rods. Moore moved St. Nick's visits to Christmas Eve; equipped him with a beer belly, a sleigh, and eight reindeer; and dropped Sinter Klaas' darker side. Moore's poem, Nissenbaum writes, was intended to help turn Christmas from a public to a private holiday, to make it an event that rich and poor families would celebrate around their fireplaces.

And it worked. By the mid–19th century, Santa Claus and the domestic Christmas were embedded in the American psyche. Over the decades, the Santa myth grew by accretion, adding layer after layer of sweet detail. In the mid–19th century, Thomas Nast's drawings defined Santa as fat, jolly, bearded, and red-suited. At the same time, Santa's home moved from Europe to the North Pole. Mrs. Claus appeared in 1899. In 1939, a copywriter for Montgomery

Ward added Rudolph to the reindeer pack. The store distributed 2.4 million copies of "Rudolph the Red-Nosed Reindeer" that year, and another 3.5 million when it reissued the story seven years later. (Santa, of course, was a commercial figure from the beginning. Store owners appropriated his picture for ads and posters.)

Throughout the 19th century and for most of the 20th century, Santa was both beloved and respected. America repelled every effort to knock him off the pantheon. In 1897, for example, a girl named Virginia O'Hanlon wrote a letter to the *New York Sun*: Her friends had told her that Santa Claus didn't exist. The *Sun* replied with one of the most famous editorials in American history: "Virginia, your little friends are wrong. They have been affected by the skepticism of a skeptical age. . . . Yes, Virginia, there is a Santa Claus. He exists as certainly as love and generosity and devotion exist." (1997 marked the centennial of "Yes, Virginia," and the editorial was much reprinted.) In the '20s and '30s, U.S. judges even issued court rulings affirming Santa Claus' existence.

But we have been affected by the skepticism of a skeptical age. Or perhaps it's the irony of an ironical age. Santa hasn't disappeared, but he's been made ridiculous. The assault by fundamentalists, Hollywood, and paranoid parents has taken its toll. His public image has degraded. Our Santa is unappetizing, a mall pedophile or a fat buffoon.

There should and can be another kind of Santa for today. In an age that valorizes family and capitalism, Santa should be recognized as a champion of both. He has been married to the same woman for 107 years. He operates a fabulously successful toy factory. It has a package delivery system that makes Federal Express look like the Pony Express. Long before the Americans with Disabilities Act, Santa staffed his factory with undersized elves.

Santa is a role model for our ambitious children, the perfect benevolent tycoon. Santa works all year round, then gives away everything he made. This should be the Santa for our time: a Soros of the North Pole, Santa the philanthropist.

Winnie-the-Pooh

The bear belongs to America.

BY DAVID PLOTZ

THE BRITISH, whose two principal hobbies seem to be slobbering over small animals and waxing nostalgic about their past, not long ago found a way to do both. They demanded the repatriation of Winnie-the-Pooh.

A British MP, Gwyneth Dunwoody, a Pol of Very Little Brain, visited the five original Pooh dolls displayed in the New York Public Library. Dunwoody beseeched the United States to liberate the "Pooh Five" from their "glass prison" and send them home. The dolls, she said, were America's Elgin marbles, a cultural treasure stolen from overseas.

(Pooh lives in a climate-controlled glass case at the library with Tigger, Piglet, Kanga, and Eeyore. The five toys used to belong to author A.A. Milne's son Christopher Robin and were the inspirations for *Winnie-the-Pooh* and *The House at Pooh Corner*. Where is Roo, you ask? When he was a child, Christopher Robin lost him in an apple orchard. That was a sad day in the Milne home.)

Within 48 hours, Pooh had made the front page of the *New York Post*; New York Gov. George Pataki had told Dunwoody to buzz off; Rep. Nita Lowey, D-N.Y., had introduced a congressional resolution declaring that the "Brits have their head in a honey jar if they think they are taking Pooh out of New York City"; The mayor brought Pooh a jar of honey and praised him as "the very best in immigration"; and the spokesman for the president of the United States had called the idea of Pooh's repatriation "unbearable." (This was, believe it or not, one of the week's better puns.) British Prime Minister Tony Blair, recognizing that discretion is the better part of absurdity, relented and withdrew Dunwoody's demand. The "special relationship" between the United States and the United Kingdom was saved.

There's no doubt that the law favors the American side in the Pooh flap. Pooh and friends have been here since 1947, when author A.A. Milne loaned them to his American publisher, E.P. Dutton, for a publicity tour. When Milne died in 1956, Dutton bought the dolls from his estate for $2,500. Pooh hero/Milne son Christopher Robin Milne expressed his satisfaction with Pooh's American home before his own death in 1995.

The law favors the Americans, but does justice? To whom does Winnie-the-Pooh belong, morally?

There are two camps in the Pooh feud: nativist and internationalist. The nativist (Dunwoody) logic: Pooh was born in Britain in 1926, his creator A.A. Milne was British, his owner Christopher Robin was British, he was raised in Britain's Hundred Acre Wood, and he played Poohsticks in a British river. Ergo, Pooh is an Englishman (Englishbear, whatever). Americans counter with an internationalist view: Pooh is a "citizen of the world," as Rudy Giuliani put it. Hundred Acre Wood is not identifiably British. What kind of English forest has a wild kangaroo and a tiger? Besides, say the internationalists, Milne's language is universally charming ("a Wedged Bear in Great Tightness"), and his moral lessons are universally applicable (if you visit a friend and gorge yourself on honey, you are likely to end up stuck in his doorway for a week while he uses your legs as a towel rack—how true!).

But there is a third view of Pooh: that he is neither British nor global. He is American. If you could summarize what an American is (or a Brit's idea of what an American is), it would be Pooh. He is a Very American Sort of Bear, a bear without a single English quality. Like the pioneers of the Old West, Pooh is endlessly greedy, and he is cunning in pursuit of that greed. *Winnie-the-Pooh* is, at bottom, the story of Pooh's quest for honey (honey = money?). His appetite cannot be sated. He eats Rabbit's honey; he eats the honey meant for the Heffalump trap; he eats the honey that is Eeyore's birthday present; he tries to eat a beehive's honey. Pooh is naive and ignorant: He spells poorly ("honey" is "hunny"), and he is impressed by the pretentious wisdom of Owl. But when it comes to avarice, Pooh has a native intelligence. He can't reach a beehive by climbing, so he jury-rigs a balloon to raid the hive from the air. Owl and Eeyore, the two most obviously British characters, are talkers. Pooh is a doer.

Pooh's greed is tempered by an all-American friendliness. Of Britain's most memorable children's-book characters—Toad and Badger in *The Wind in the Willows*, Aslan in the "Narnia" books, Alice and the Mad Hatter in *Alice's Adventures in Wonderland*—Pooh is by far the sunniest. There is no dark side to Pooh, no complicated European soul. Pooh is guileless, blithe, good-natured, democratic. He is the best friend to all. (There is also a brash self-confidence to Pooh: He composes songs of praise to himself that would have done Whitman proud. After rescuing Piglet from drowning, Pooh sings: "Three Cheers for Pooh! (For Who?) For Pooh—(Why what did he do?) I thought you knew; He saved his friend from a wetting! Three Cheers for Bear!")

Pooh's world, too, is far more American than British. Hundred Acre Wood resembles an idealized vision of America's pioneer past, a wild, empty land populated by a few hardy pioneers who band together when danger threatens (Heffalumps!).

And Pooh belongs to America for economic reasons as well as literary ones. Where would he be today without American commercial know-how? For the first 50 years of his life, Pooh was a modest franchise—a pair of books that sold fairly well to British and American parents. America rescued him from minor cult status and gave him to the world (at a not-insignificant profit). Pooh has now sold more than 20 million books, most of them in the

United States. Penguin, which holds the U.S. copyright on the original Pooh books, has published black-and-white Pooh books, color Pooh books, miniature Pooh "storybooks," Pooh in Latin (*Winnie ille Pu*), Pooh for New Agers (*The Tao of Pooh* and its companion volume, *The Te of Piglet*), and even Pooh for managers.

Disney, which owns Pooh's merchandising rights, has done even more to spread his gospel. Disney has produced half a dozen animated features, one of which won an Academy Award. It has also aired countless episodes of *The New Adventures of Winnie the Pooh*. "Disney Pooh" horrifies Pooh traditionalists ("abhorrent," says one young mother I know). He wears a red jacket ("Classic Pooh" was naked) and speaks with an American accent. He fights movie monsters, sings in a musical Western, and celebrates Thanksgiving (Thanksgiving?). But Disney Pooh reaches the world. Pooh videos from Disney have sold nearly tens of millions of copies, and Disney Pooh decorates books, blankets, albums, bedding, slippers, calendars, backpacks, and cookie jars sold to impressionable children everywhere. Disney makes $5 billion a year off Pooh, making the bear the most valuable character in the world. He's so lucrative that Disney spent a decade in a Byzantine, mammoth lawsuit over Pooh merchandising rights—a legal fight involving seamy private detectives, dumpster diving, and practically every lawyer on the West Coast. When Pooh is in a billion-dollar lawsuit, you know he's really American.

The Gillette Man

A close shave for a great American.

BY BRYAN CURTIS

WHEN PROCTER & GAMBLE announced that it had purchased Gillette, manufacturer of the world's best-selling line of men's razors, in January 2005, nothing short of manhood was at stake. The manhood belonged to of one of TV's most enduring icons: the Gillette man. Through dozens of commercials over dozens of years, we have gleaned a few immutable truths about the Gillette man. For instance, he shows a great affinity for two-handed cheek massage. He prefers women who stroll up behind him with their midriffs wrapped in towels. He always shaves after he styles his hair, which, incidentally, is an unwavering shade of light brown. For a playboy, the Gillette man has genuine heart. In recent ads, he's been seen sharing meaningful grooming moments with his father and tending lovingly to his infant son.

But the Gillette man harbors a dirty little secret. His "best a man can get" boast is nothing but a brave facade. Shaving is his great humiliation—the man at his very worst. He dreads gruesome shaving injuries: jagged flesh cuts and red bumps that sprout up at his neckline. He vows to shave more slowly and precisely, but he continues to slather on foaming gel and slice his blade carelessly against the grain. The enduring genius of Gillette man is that he somehow dignifies these vulnerabilities and then banishes them with a splash of machismo.

The Gillette man derives his swagger from the company's founder, King Camp Gillette, who began tinkering with men's razors in 1895. King Gillette was a turn-of-century archetype: half visionary, half crank. An unapologetic utopian—he wanted the entire American population to move to a bustling city on the shores of Lake Ontario—Gillette entertained a utopian vision in men's shaving. He noticed that men had to constantly sharpen their razors, which would dull after only a few uses. So he conceived of a line of cheap, disposable razor blades that could be purchased in bulk and discarded before they ever needed sharpening. After a shaky start, the Gillette Safety Razor Co. grew into an iconic brand and helped usher in the age of disposable goods. The wrapping around each blade contained King Gillette's likeness, printed, as *Fortune Small Business* noted, in the color of money. During World War I, King Gillette sold his shavers to the U.S. government, branding thousands upon thousands of soldiers as lifelong customers.

Decades after King Gillette's death in 1932, the Gillette man became the public face of the company. At first, the Gillette man was a strapping guy-next-door, obsessed with self-betterment and team sports. His slogan was "Look sharp! Feel sharp! Be sharp!" The company lent its name to every sporting venture it could find, from the 1939 World Series to the New England Patriots' new stadium in Foxborough, Mass. Occasionally, the Gillette pitchmen were real athletes like Muhammad Ali or David Beckham, who provided aspirational examples of the masculine ideal.

The Gillette man should have become an iconic figure of the Me Decade. Instead, the 1980s found him at his lowest ebb. The company was rocked by three hostile takeover bids from Revlon's Ron Perelman. The Gillette business model, which was built around manufacturing high-quality razors, was rendered obsolete by the appearance of Bic's new disposable razors, which allowed you to throw away both the razor and the blade. As if to prove that art must imitate life, even the Gillette man's commercials became great embarrassments. In a 1983 ad, the Gillette man was depicted as the tiny weakling on a basketball court full of giants; his shaver, he said, helped him even the odds. The previous year, the Gillette man was rendered to look like the actor Anthony Michael Hall, wearing a pinstriped bathrobe and yelping, "I like it!" after every razor stroke.

He recovered some of his dignity in 1990, when Gillette moved the market away from disposable razors, unveiling the Sensor and then, eight years later, its most iconic razor, the Mach 3. As *The New Yorker* reported, the plating of the Mach 3 was modeled after the shape-shifting villain in *Terminator* 2, and the razor's unveiling lent the Gillette man a Schwarzeneggerian swagger. The Gillette man once again became a virile playboy. He dumped the bathrobe for the shirtless look and took up extreme sports like mountain-climbing. In a commercial that ran during the 2004 Super Bowl, the Gillette man attempted to describe his Weltanschauung: "You know the feelin'. Every guy's had it. You're unbeatable. Unstoppable. You got that walkin'-on-water feelin'. . . . And once you've had the feelin', you want it back. There's nothin' like it. It's the best. . . . Every move is smooth. Every word is cool. Yeah. I never want to lose that feelin'. It's the best, man."

Beneath the macho bluster, though, the Gillette man was embracing a 1990s ideal of manhood. Gillette wanted to move beyond sports iconography and depict the best moments in a man's life—marriage, children, even religion. Gillette ads began to feature father-son fishing trips and joyous family weddings. The 2004 Super Bowl ad contains a tender, almost heavenly image. Amid the shots of astronauts and soccer players, the viewer suddenly notices an ethereal white light. Why, it's an angel! And not the Gillette man's girlfriend, either. A real, honest-to-goodness angel, come to bless his daily grooming rituals. This revealed an intriguing and heretofore unknown side of the Gillette man. Was he an enthusiastic Christian? A fan of Tony Kushner?

Lately, the Gillette man has embraced another masculine ideal: trading up. The Gillette company has mastered the art of releasing a new, more innovative razor every few years, whether humanity needs it or not. The Atra became the Atra Plus. The Sensor yielded to the Sensor Excel. After six years of market dominance, the excellent Mach 3 gave way to the M3 Power, a razor that requires an AAA battery to "micro-pulse" hairs into an upright and locked position. The unveiling of a Gillette razor has become as routine as the release of a new model sports car. A financial analyst told the *Boston Globe* that Gillette's strategy was "not revolutionary, it's evolutionary."

But in 2005, the Procter & Gamble sale seemed to pose a threat to the Gillette man. It was a shotgun wedding of the grooming categories. Just as Gillette dominates men's shaving products, Procter & Gamble provides the top toiletry brands for women: Tampax, Olay, Cover Girl, and Max Factor. Would Procter & Gamble's femininity sap the Gillette man of machismo? You know the feelin'. Every guy's had it. First you're in love. Smitten. But then you're married. Trapped. You've got that stuck-in-jail feelin'. It's the worst, man. The worst.

Tarzan

How we have turned Burroughs' Ape-Man into a Momma's Boy.

BY MICHAEL LIND

CARL JUNG ONCE OBSERVED that it is easier to discern the presence of archetypes from the collective subconscious in works of pulp fiction by writers such as H. Rider Haggard than it is in literary masterpieces. If only Jung had put Edgar Rice Burroughs on his depth-psychologist's couch. Burroughs was the George Lucas of his day, creating in Tarzan and other characters beings as profoundly mythical—and as stereotypically superficial—as Darth Vader. Like Luke Skywalker's saga, the tale of Tarzan mixes and matches motifs from the archetype-haunted dreamtime of humanity anatomized by Jung and Jung's disciple, Joseph Campbell. The tale of the prince raised in secret by adopted parents (King Arthur, Luke Skywalker) is fused with the story of the feral child raised by animals (Romulus and Remus, Enkidu, Mowgli, Pecos Bill) in the romance of the orphaned English lord raised by a foster family of African apes.

The fact that Tarzan is really an English lord—Lord Greystoke, to be precise—was central to Burroughs' conception of his character. In the pulp fiction of Burroughs, as in pulp fiction of any period, timeless archetypes rub shoulders with the vulgar prejudices of the writer and his audience. In the works of Burroughs, today's race/class/gender theorists can easily find a key to the racial, social, and sexual anxieties of early 20th-century white American men and boys. When the first Tarzan books were published, the British Empire ruled the waves, the United States had recently joined the ranks of imperial powers, and white supremacy was the norm in the United States and throughout the world. Confidence in the innate superiority of the Caucasian race—and, within that race, of its Anglo-Saxon variant—coexisted with paranoia about the yellow peril and black "savagery."

The two major characters in the oeuvre of Edgar Rice Burroughs are Tarzan of the Apes and John Carter of Mars. Although John Carter never made it in Hollywood the way that his cousin in the jungle jockstrap did, it is worth reviving him to make a point. Tarzan and John Carter were both exemplars of Anglo-Saxon masculinity—Tarzan, the heir to an aristocratic English family, and John Carter, an upper-class Virginian by birth. The Tarzan and Carter stories can be viewed as experiments—take a member of the Anglo-Saxon ruling class, strip him of all his advantages, and put him in a radically different environment, in order that the innate superiority of his breed may be demonstrated. Whether in Africa (the symbol of precivilized savagery) or on an old, desiccated Mars (the symbol of overrefinement and cultural exhaustion), the Anglo-Saxon man proves that he is royalty. Tarzan becomes Lord of the Jungle, John Carter weds the Princess of Mars. Space, in Burroughs, is a metaphor for time. Tarzan and John Carter represent the era of Anglo-American civilization, at the midpoint between prehistoric barbarism and post-historic decadence.

Burroughs' genius can be seen in the way that he redeemed the imagery of savagery for his Anglo-Saxon ape-man. In the mythology of white supremacy, even before Charles Darwin, black Africans and other non-whites were assimilated to apes (Thomas Jefferson, in his *Notes on the State of Virginia*, finds credible the rumor that African women mate with orangutans). In much 19th- and early 20th-century pulp fiction, American Indians and black Americans have a mystical rapport with animals, which author and audience alike understood arose from their proximity on the evolutionary scale. But Burroughs' Tarzan is closer to the animals than the black Africans who live nearby. The Great White Hope is at once more civilized and more savage than the "natives"—he is the Lone Ranger and Tonto. With Tarzan monopolizing the highest and lowest rungs of the Chain of Being, the "natives" find themselves deprived of the one asset that racist mythology attributed to them, closeness to the animals, leaving them without any particular function in the economy of kitsch literature, except to be rescued by Tarzan from rogue elephants and the occasional witch doctor.

When first published, the Tarzan stories provided a largely American audience of white men and boys with a fantasy version of the ultimate White Guy, the virile aristocrat, who, far from being effete and degenerate, could go Ape as well as Ascot. Something like this vision inspired Theodore Roosevelt, the asthmatic Yankee patrician who turned himself into a cowboy and, as an ex-president, nearly died while exploring a tributary of the Amazon in Brazil, in an adventure that might have been scripted by Burroughs. George H.W. Bush—a professed admirer of TR—is the Tarzan of our day: A patrician Yalie (Lord Greystoke), and at the same time a Texan redneck (Tarzan), engaged in wildcatting (could there be a more metaphorically resonant term?). By jumping out of airplanes in his 70s, Bush continues to battle the Wimp Factor. Perhaps he should swing from vines as well. By contrast, George W., a rich kid who, unlike his father, sat out the war of his generation, is Boy.

The Tarzan mythos, then, depends on a balance of tensions—between Tarzan the Ape-Man and Lord Greystoke, between England and Africa, between civilization and savagery. Play down one side of the equation, and the meaning of this whole system of pre-World War II social stereotypes collapses.

This is what happened when Hollywood got hold of the Tarzan story. Beginning with the Johnny Weissmuller films, the jungle began eclipsing the English manor. Tarzan became simply a feral child, a white Mowgli. The genre changed to pastoral: Tarzan and Jane became the equivalents of the innocent shepherds and shepherdesses of Hellenistic Greek and Renaissance pastoral fiction, striving to preserve their natural idyll from corruption by civilization. Pastoral Tarzan need not be an English lord. He need not even be white. A black or brown or Asian Tarzan would defeat the whole point of the Burroughs mythos but would not be out of place in the Hollywood or TV versions.

Disney's animated *Tarzan* (and Disney's new Broadway *Tarzan*) is the politically correct heir of several generations of Hollywood Tarzans—a facsimile of a facsimile. Gone is the social Darwinist worldview that underpinned the original. In the prologue we see Tarzan's parents, but we do not learn they are titled. Indeed, from their facility at assembling a tree house we might think that they are, not Lord and Lady Greystoke, but Mr. and Mrs. Robinson (as in Crusoe or Swiss Family). The embarrassing problem of what to do with the "natives" in a post-racist age is solved by eliminating the natives altogether. Disney's gorillas live in a jungle uninhabited by human beings, until Europeans intrude.

The Disneyfied Tarzan is such a wimp that he is not allowed to kill anything or anybody, although our Paleolithic pacifist is permitted to use martial arts techniques in self-defense. The two villains of the movie are a homicidal (and simiocidal) cheetah and an English hunter—the Evil White Male without which no PC epic would be complete. But when the time comes for them to die, both do themselves in accidentally while fighting Tarzan: The cheetah falls atop a spearhead that Tarzan happens to be holding, and the Englishman inadvertently hangs himself on jungle vines.

In *The Epic of Gilgamesh*, a prostitute lures Enkidu away from his animal companions. Once he has slept with a woman, the animals refuse to associate with him; he cannot go home again. Masculine wildness is overcome by civilized femininity. In Disney's *Tarzan* film, nature is feminine and civilization masculine.

Disney's *Tarzan* is not only post-imperial, post-racist, and post-classist but also post-masculine. Tarzan is a momma's boy. His gorilla foster mother, Kala, remains on the scene after he reaches adulthood. When Tarzan introduces Jane to Kala, he grovels and whimpers before a disapproving Ma Gorilla.

Halfway through the film, Tarzan, a Victorian-era Enkidu, lured by Jane, is prepared to follow her back to England. But then, having learned how evil civilized Englishmen can be, Tarzan, Jane, and her father (in the PC universe, old and feeble white men are tolerable) decide to renounce civilized society for the jungle. There, by happy coincidence, the two alpha males (Kerchak the bull ape and the evil English hunter) are gone, clearing the way for the utopia of beta males and females. Although Tarzan is now nominally in control, one suspects that Kala the Ape-Mom, the Empress Dowager of the Jungle, is really in charge. At movie's end, Tarzan and Jane move in with Mom and her furry family, like '90s yuppies who have given up and moved back home. Perhaps Jane's widowed human father will wed Tarzan's widowed gorilla mother (so the Southern Baptist Convention should be worried about bestiality but not homosexuality).

If the pulp fiction of Edgar Rice Burroughs gives us a glimpse into the often appalling collective unconscious of white-supremacist America, the Disney version of *Tarzan* will provide a similar service to future scholars pondering the equally weird mentality of feminized and Green America, in the early years of the 21st century. If the original *Tarzan* celebrated the Anglo-Saxon male proving his superiority over Nature [red in tooth and claw,] Disney's version embodies the ideology that vilifies the "white male" and idealizes the feminine (human and ape) and the wilderness imagined by customers of The Nature Store. Me, Tarzan. You, Jane. Nature Good. Civilization Bad. Girls good. Boys bad.

Rumor has it that a future object of touchy-feely bowdlerization by Disney is *Beowulf*. No doubt in the Disney version, Beowulf and the feisty, coed-army warrior-princess who inevitably will be written into the script as his partner will befriend a misunderstood Grendel and Grendel's mom (it's not easy being green). Disney is evil—not because it's turning children into liberals, but because it's turning them into wimps.

Scooby-Doo

Hey, dog! How do you do the voodoo that you do so well?

BY CHRIS SUELLENTROP

HERE'S THE EASIEST WAY to comprehend the longevity of *Scooby-Doo*: Casey Kasem has been doing the voice of Shaggy (Norville Rogers, if you insist on his given name) for longer than he hosted his weekly top 40 radio show. He started voicing Shaggy in 1969, the year before *American Top 40* debuted, and he's still got the part, on television in *What's New Scooby-Doo?* and in the direct-to-video movies the franchise keeps churning out.

Though it's hard to believe—and for animation purists, practically impossible to stomach—*Scooby-Doo* is the most enduringly popular cartoon in TV history. Starting with the original *Scooby-Doo, Where Are You!*, the show, in various permutations, was produced for 17 years (and, with its latest incarnation, it's in production again), making it the longest-running network cartoon ever. Because of syndication, it's never been off the air since it debuted, and it probably never will be. The empire has expanded to include the 2002 feature film *Scooby-Doo*, which raked in $153 million at the box office and was followed in 2004 by *Scooby-Doo 2: Monsters Unleashed*, the second of what promises to be *many* live-action *Scooby* movies.

Acknowledging *Scooby*'s durability is easier than explaining it. *Scooby-Doo* wormed its way into the culture through years of drip-drip accretion. It's the Cal Ripken of cartoons: Not the best, though certainly not the worst, it just shows up day after day after day, and you end up loving it for that.

For years, not even the show's creators at Hanna-Barbera—the first TV animation studio and the inventors of "limited animation" (that is, animation cheap enough for TV-size budgets)—realized the appeal of *Scooby-Doo*. Instead, *The Flintstones*, or even *The Jetsons*, was thought to be the studio's flagship property. The 1989 50th anniversary TV special for Hanna-Barbera was dubbed "A Yabba Dabba Do Celebration."

But Bedrock might as well be the, uh, Stone Age for today's young audiences, while the gang at *Scooby-Doo* maintains its hypnotic appeal. The eponymous dog star's Q rating tops Bugs Bunny's among kids. The franchise's direct-to-video titles consistently hit the best-seller lists. (And yes, in a nod to changing times, Scooby, Shaggy, and Fred do DVD commentary.) Kid-oriented *Scooby*-licensed video games have been popular since the mid-'90s. In 2000, *Scooby-Doo* won a mock presidential election held by the Cartoon Network, which still airs an hour-and-a-half of *Scooby* shows each weekday. Unlike the evening "Adult Swim" fare, the Cartoon Network's daytime audience is dominated by tykes. One key to understanding *Scooby* is to realize it has never performed the double-ironic back flip that would make it an adult phenomenon. It has always appealed first to little kids.

One early hint of the show's hold on children came in February 1971, when the BBC pulled *Scooby-Doo, Where Are You!* from the air, and 70 Scottish children staged a protest outside the Beeb's Scotland headquarters. An employee recently told the Scottish *Daily Record* that the protest remains the biggest at that BBC location's history. But beyond making comparisons to the Hardy Boys and Nancy Drew, or citing the general appeal of talking dogs, or noting that Daphne is as sexualized as a kiddie cartoon character gets, it's difficult to say exactly why the show has had such a long-standing appeal. It's not as if the show's animator, Iwao Takamoto—his other creations include the Great Gazoo of *The*

Flintstones and Grape Ape—is an unheralded genius, a mystery-genre Tex Avery or Walt Disney. "I never got it," complained Mitchell Kriegman, the creator of Nickelodeon's *Clarissa Explains It All*, to the *Boston Globe* a few years back. "It's got kind of a slacker appeal, a no-resistance story line." Animators and children's TV creators around the world must see *Scooby* and ask themselves: Why can't my crappy show become iconic?

Jim Millan, the writer-director of *Scooby-Doo in StageFright—Live on Stage* (yes, there was a touring theatrical production of *Scooby-Doo*) tried to engage in some bigthink about the show's popularity during publicity interviews. "They like Scooby's enthusiasm for life," he theorized to the *Baltimore Sun*. "It represents a youthful, optimistic America, where you can solve a problem with good intentions." To the *Toronto Star*, Millan compared *Scooby-Doo* to 19th-century European commedia dell'arte, with its stock characters and costumes. "Scooby and Shaggy love to eat," Millan said. "But the delight is in seeing the permutations." To Nashville's *Tennessean*, Millan said of Scooby, "He symbolizes youth, in a way."

TV snobs surely see *Scooby*'s ineffable charms as another brick in the wall of American decline, the latest example of how we're all slouching toward Toon Town. As if our children should all be watching *The Sopranos*. Maybe *Scooby*'s appeal makes sense when you compare it to the rest of kids' TV. The most ham-handed of children's shows try to stuff a moral message down the audience's throat. But the moral code of *Scooby-Doo* permeates the entire enterprise without you ever noticing it. The *Washington Post*'s Hank Stuever concisely elucidated the "*Scooby* worldview" when the first live-action movie came out: "Kids should meddle, dogs are sweet, life is groovy, and if something scares you, you should confront it." What needs to be explained about that?

SHANGRI-LAS

VH1

The surreal network.

BY BRYAN CURTIS

AS A CABLE NETWORK, VH1 arrived too early for its own good. Christened "Video Hits 1" in 1985, the network spent the better part of its first decade desperately looking for ways to outflank MTV—it was "MTV for Old People" during its adult-contemporary phase, when the network seemed to be a shrine to Phil Collins, and, later and more charitably, it was "MTV With Music Videos." It's ironic that this dreary period in VH1's history is the one the network chooses to revisit—again and again—in recent shows like *I Love the 80s, I Love the 80s Strikes Back*, and the *40 Most Awesomely Bad Break-Up Songs. . . Ever*. It's like a twenty-something leafing through his high-school yearbook and wondering what might have been. To understand the much-heralded renaissance of VH1, in which the network has gone from unwatchable to strangely riveting, the place to start is with its inferiority complex.

After years in the adult-contemporary ghetto, VH1 showed the first signs of a new attitude with *Pop-Up Video*, the series that debuted in 1996. With cheeky info-bubbles interrupting music videos, the show was subtly anticipating two values that would shape the new VH1. First, there was the obsession with commenting on pop culture. Second was that in order to be a success, VH1 was going to have to adopt the pose of an outsider. Unlike MTV, which cozied up to celebrities lest they skip the Video Music Awards, VH1 was distinctly B-list. And rather than trying conventional methods to improve its status—such as moving into new genres or attempting noble pop scholarship like *Behind the Music*—VH1 began to exult in its second-tier status. If MTV was going to be the A-list star, VH1 would become the heckler on the rope line, the hyperarticulate commentator on pop.

VH1 executives like to talk about the network's "voice"—the one that has been adopted by its hosts, pop commentators, and announcer. Affectionate and highly ironic, the voice sounds a bit like a gentle imitation of Chuck Klosterman. It is the kind of voice that would thoroughly dismantle a Madonna video, pointing out the gratuitous excess and the cheesiness of the mise-en-scène, before admitting, "But wasn't it *great*?" VH1 cultivated this voice in *I Love the 80s* (2002), a show in which hipster comedians riffed on a decade's worth of pop, cracking wise on everything from INXS to Child's Play. (Dee Snider: "It's a doll! Step on it! It's over!") In recent years, VH1 has developed two types of nostalgia programming. There is reflective nostalgia, like *I Love the 80s*. Then there is what you might call "instant" nostalgia: *Best Week Ever*, in which a cast of comedians riffs on the last six days, and more recently *Web Junk 20*, which surveys stuff that's going around on the Internet. Turning the pop present into instant nostalgia keeps the network fresh, explains Michael Hirschorn, VH1's executive vice president of original programming and production.

These days, VH1's sister network is not MTV. It is ESPN. In ESPN's freewheeling early days—back in the 1980s, before it became a sprawling sports empire—the network had the feel of an exclusive boys club. *SportsCenter* anchors were minor celebrities, playing to young males who shared a set of cultural references (years of accumulated sports detritus), and more frequent viewing let you in on the inside jokes. VH1 aims for a similar appeal. Hipster comedians (Michael Ian Black, Hal Sparks) replace hipster sports anchors, and the furrowed-brow sports debates have become meditations on extinct TV, nearly forgotten music, and the most awesomely bad breakup songs ever. VH1's ideal viewer, like

ESPN's, is a male in his late 20s nursing a pop hangover, and the comedians are his spiritual gurus. To further the "just us guys" aesthetic, VH1 gives its shows (which can cost a fortune to produce because of rights fees) a kind of low-fi authenticity that contrasts with MTV's slicker productions. "Part of the VH1 approach is having it look tossed off, when in fact it isn't," says Hirschorn.

The network's other chief interest, in its new identity, is reality TV, which it calls "celebreality." Here, VH1 displays the same cheeky indifference toward celebrity and walks the same thin line between nostalgic affection and outright ridicule. As a rule, the "celebrities" that pop up on VH1 are not, and usually never were, big stars. They are niche types (Hulk Hogan), nobodies (Wendy the Snapple Lady), and has-beens on the verge of an emotional breakdown (Danny Bonaduce). The network's reality shows exist to show what desperate lengths they will go to revive their careers. VH1 is the network where a has-been will submit to live in a house with other has-beens (*The Surreal Life*), go to a fat camp (*Celebrity Fit Club*), or endure a prolonged and excruciating emotional crisis (*Breaking Bonaduce*). It is riveting television, and more than a little bit cruel. Having been exhumed as kitsch icons on *I Love the 80s*, the has-beens are now taking turns being smirked at in the flesh.

So, is VH1 any good? Well, whatever joy *I Love the 80s* once elicited, it's safe to say the network has strip-mined the last three decades for all they're worth. ("We're nearer to the end of that than we are to the beginning," says Hirschorn.) And if the house comedians seem to have been a little flat as of late, the network can still turn out genuinely brilliant television, like *TV's Illest Minority Moments* (2004), which highlighted the racism that regularly infiltrates network TV. The celebreality shows, I'm forced to admit, are uniformly good. And then there's Flavor Flav, the former "hype man" of Public Enemy, whose recent renaissance is due to his permanence on VH1. Withered and scratchy-voiced (he's like a corporeal embodiment of a has-been), Flavor has lately gone searching for a romantic partner on the show *Flavor of Love*. He seems caught somewhere between his own nostalgia and the pop present, between finding new dignity and lapsing into self-parody—he is, in short, the perfect celebrity spokesman for VH1.

Whole Foods

The dark secrets of the organic-food movement.

BY FIELD MALONEY

IT'S HARD TO FIND FAULT with Whole Foods, the haute-crunchy supermarket chain that has made a fortune by transforming grocery shopping into a bright and shiny, progressive experience. Indeed, the road to wild profits and cultural cachet has been surprisingly smooth for the supermarket chain. It gets mostly sympathetic coverage in the local and national media, and red-carpet treatment from the communities it enters. But does Whole Foods have an Achilles' heel? And more important, does the organic movement itself, whose coattails Whole Foods has ridden to such success, have dark secrets of its own?

Granted, there's plenty that's praiseworthy about Whole Foods. John Mackey, the company's chairman, likes to say, "There's no inherent reason why business cannot be ethical, socially responsible, and profitable." And under the umbrella creed of "sustainability," Whole Foods pays its workers a solid living wage—its lowest earners average $13.15 an hour—with excellent benefits and health care. No executive, not even the CEO, makes more than 14 times the employee average. In early 2006, Whole Foods announced that it had committed to buying a year's supply of power from a wind-power utility in Wyoming.

But even if Whole Foods has a happy staff and nice windmills, is it really as virtuous as it seems? Take the produce section, usually located in the geographic center of the shopping floor and the spiritual heart of a Whole Foods outlet. (Every media profile of the company invariably contains a paragraph of fawning produce porn, near-sonnets about "gleaming melons" and "glistening kumquats.") In the produce section of Whole Foods' flagship New York City store at the Time Warner Center, shoppers browse under a big banner that lists "Reasons To Buy Organic." On the banner, the first heading is "Save Energy." The accompanying text explains how organic farmers, who use natural fertilizers like manure and compost, avoid the energy waste involved in the manufacture of synthetic fertilizers. It's a technical point that probably barely registers with most shoppers but contributes to a vague sense of virtue.

Fair enough. But here's another technical point that Whole Foods fails to mention and that highlights what has gone wrong with the organic-food movement in the last couple of decades. Let's say you live in New York City and want to buy a pound of tomatoes in season. Say you can choose between conventionally grown New Jersey tomatoes or organic ones grown in Chile. Of course, the New Jersey tomatoes will be cheaper. They will also almost certainly be fresher, having traveled a fraction of the distance. But which is the more eco-conscious choice? In terms of energy savings, there's no contest: Just think of the fossil fuels expended getting those organic tomatoes from Chile. Which brings us to the question: Setting aside freshness, price, and energy conservation, should a New Yorker just instinctively choose organic, even if the produce comes from Chile? A tough decision, but you can make a self-interested case for the social and economic benefit of going Jersey, especially if you prefer passing fields of tomatoes to fields of condominiums when you tour the Garden State.

Another heading on the Whole Foods banner says "Help the Small Farmer." "Buying organic," it states, "supports the small, family farmers that make up a large percentage of organic food producers." This is semantic sleight of hand. As one small family farmer in Connecticut told me, "Almost all the organic food in this country comes out of California. And five or six big California farms dominate the whole industry." There's a widespread misperception in this country—one that organic growers, no matter how giant, happily encourage—that "organic" means "small family farmer." That hasn't been the case for years, certainly not since 1990, when the Department of Agriculture drew up its official guidelines for organic food. Whole Foods knows this well, and so the line about the "small family farmers that make up a large percentage of organic food producers" is sneaky. There are a lot of small, family-run organic farmers, but their share of the organic crop in this country, and of the produce sold at Whole Foods, is minuscule.

A nearby banner at the Time Warner Center Whole Foods proclaims "Our Commitment to the Local Farmer," but this also doesn't hold up to scrutiny. More likely, the burgeoning local-food movement is making Whole Foods uneasy. After all, a multinational chain can't promote a "buy local" philosophy without being self-defeating. When I made an autumn visit to Whole Foods—high season for native fruits and vegetables on the East Coast—only a token amount of local produce was on display. What Whole Foods does do for local farmers is hang glossy pinups throughout the store, what they call "grower profiles," which depict tousled, friendly looking organic farmers standing in front of their crops. During one winter Whole Foods drop-by, the only local produce for sale was a shelf of upstate apples, but the grower profiles were still up. There was a picture of a sandy-haired organic leek farmer named Dave, from Whately, Mass., above a shelf of conventionally grown yellow onions from Oregon. Another profile showed a guy named Ray Rex munching on an ear of sweet corn he grew on his generations-old, picturesque organic acres. The photograph was pinned above a display of conventionally grown white onions from Mexico.

These profiles may be heartwarming, but they also artfully mislead customers about what they're paying premium prices for. If Whole Foods marketing didn't revolve so much around explicit (as well as subtly suggestive) appeals to food ethics, it'd be easier to forgive some exaggerations and distortions.

Of course, above and beyond social and environmental ethics, and even taste, people buy organic food because they believe that it's better for them. All things being equal, food grown without pesticides is healthier for you. But American populism chafes against the notion of good health for those who can afford it. Charges of elitism—media wags, in otherwise flattering profiles, have called Whole Foods "Whole Paycheck" and "wholesome, healthy for the wholesome, wealthy"—are the only criticism of Whole Foods that seems to have stuck. Which brings us to a new kid in the organic-food sandbox: Wal-Mart, the world's biggest grocery retailer, has expanded into organic foods. If buying food grown without chemical pesticides and synthetic fertilizers has been elevated to a status-conscious lifestyle choice, it could also be transformed into a bare-bones commodity purchase.

When the Department of Agriculture established the guidelines for organic food in 1990, it blew a huge opportunity. The USDA—under heavy agribusiness lobbying—adopted an abstract set of restrictions for organic agriculture and left "local" out of the formula. What passes for organic farming today has strayed far from what the shaggy utopians who got the movement going back in the '60s and '70s had in mind. But if these pioneers dreamed of revolutionizing the nation's food supply, they surely didn't intend for organic to become a luxury item, a high-end lifestyle choice.

It's likely that neither Wal-Mart nor Whole Foods will do much to encourage local agriculture or small farming, but in an odd twist, Wal-Mart, with its simple "More for Less" credo, might do far more to democratize the nation's food supply than Whole Foods. The organic-food movement is in danger of exacerbating the growing gap between rich and poor in this country by contributing to a two-tiered national food supply, with healthy food for the rich. Could Wal-Mart's populist strategy prove to be more "sustainable" than Whole Foods? Stranger things have happened.

Al Jazeera

It's just as fair as CNN.

BY CHRIS SUELLENTROP

IN A WAR WITH NO CLEAR WINNERS so far, perhaps the only real victor has been Al Jazeera. The Arabic-language news station has been maligned by some for airing grisly footage of Iraqi civilian casualties and American POWs and for serving as a mouthpiece for al-Qaida's threatening messages to the West. But those criticisms have been overshadowed by the sympathetic coverage the Middle Eastern news network received in the 2004 documentary *Control Room* and in many American news outlets. The network once deemed the inflammatory fuel of Islamic radicalism was ultimately pronounced by the *New York Times* as "the kind of television station we should encourage." The upshot of all that encouragement: Al Jazeera is coming to America. Venerable broadcasters like the BBC's David Frost have signed on with Al Jazeera International, an English-language satellite channel that's expected to launch in 2006.

What changed? Certainly not Al Jazeera. The network still presents a pro-Arab slant on the news of the day, including the war in Iraq. A visit to the Al Jazeera Web site during the early stages of the war turned up images that portray Iraqi civilians as invaded rather than liberated: rotating photos of wounded children with patches over their eyes and blood on their faces next to a separate image of a mournful woman standing in front of rubble. This emphasis on civilian casualties is consistent with the approach the TV network has taken, according to those who have watched Al Jazeera's TV coverage in Arabic. "They focus on the casualties. They show very gruesome images of civilian casualties that we don't see on America media," says Mohammed El-Nawawy, co-author of the admiring book *Al Jazeera: How the Free Arab News Network Scooped the World and Changed the Middle East*.

So, it's not as if Al Jazeera has morphed into the news as told by Lee Greenwood. Or even that Al Jazeera has morphed into CNN. Rather, it's fairer to say that since the war began, CNN—and American TV news in general—has become more like Al Jazeera. To those who have tarred him as pro-war and pro-administration, CNN's Aaron Brown replied: "I think there is some truth in it." Fox's Neil Cavuto was blunter: "You say I wear my biases on my sleeve? Better that than pretend you have none, but show them clearly in your work." Cavuto's comments echo a statement made by Al Jazeera's Ramallah correspondent to *60 Minutes* in May 2001 about the Israeli-Palestinian conflict: "To be objective in this area is not easy because we live here. We are part of the people here. And this situation belongs to us also, and we have our opinions."

American TV news has always presented an American perspective, just as Al Jazeera presents an Arab perspective. But in wartime, the American slant has become more obvious, and as a result Al Jazeera's Arab slant has become less objectionable. In 2001, Fouad Ajami declared in a long *New York Times Magazine* article that Al Jazeera was "a dangerous force." But in the wake of this war's coverage by the American media, his fears and criticisms sound quaint. Ajami blasted the channel's "shameless" promos, including a montage of scenes that portrayed a clear sympathy for the Palestinians. But how different are MSNBC's or CNN's montages of heroic American soldiers set to patriotic, martial music? Or the recurring shots of Americans saving babies and handing out candy to children? Ajami also criticized Al Jazeera for focusing too much on the tragedy of a single individual, 12-year-old Muhamed al-Durra, a Palestinian shot and killed in Gaza. But American networks pull similar heartstring-tugging tricks, such as the mediathon over the rescue of Jessica Lynch, a single American POW. (American television ignores, for the most part, the lives and the deaths of Brits and Iraqis.)

This is not to say that Al Jazeera and American TV news are equivalents. For one thing, Al Jazeera still receives funding from the monarchical government of Qatar, and even fans like El-Nawawy rap Al Jazeera for refraining from tough coverage—or any coverage—of Qatari politics. But Al Jazeera, with its Fox-like slogan "The opinion and the other opinion," is the closest thing the Arab world has to an independent press. The network's plan for an English-language channel shows that Al Jazeera harbors a dream of becoming worldly and perhaps more mainstream.

Particularly in wartime, the best a network can hope for is what El-Nawawy and his co-author, Adel Iskandar, call "contextual objectivity"—an attempt "to reflect all sides of any story while retaining the values, beliefs and sentiments of the target audience." Based on the positive coverage in the American media, Al Jazeera is at least approaching that standard. It's telling the American side of the story, even as its sympathies clearly lie with the plight of the Iraqi people, whom the network, fairly or unfairly, sees as suffering under both Saddam Hussein and the American-led invasion to remove him.

From the opposite perspective, the U.S. networks are doing the same: giving lip service to the Arab view of the war, while endorsing the American view that the conflict is just and necessary. The war has given lie to the idea that American journalists don't have opinions. One question: Why must we return to the lie when it's time for peace?

Dunkin' Donuts

A more perfect pastry.

BY BRYAN CURTIS

SOMETHING IS AMISS at Dunkin' Donuts. The store's loyal constituents—cops, firemen, construction workers—report disturbing sightings of soy milk. *The Boston Globe* reported that the doughnut titan hired a professional chef—trained in *Europe*—to perfect its new steak, egg, and cheese sandwich, which features "a higher-quality piece of meat and scrambled eggs instead of a fried egg." Some Chicago-area Dunkin' outlets are dabbling with wireless Internet, which had previously been the domain of high-end coffee joints like Starbucks. One could be forgiven for thinking that Dunkin' Donuts, the traditional home of the blue-collar masses and purveyor of some of the most frightening fast-food on the planet, was angling for middlebrow respectability.

Dunkin' Donuts still boasts some gruesome pleasures: "The Great One," a 24-ounce coffee chalice, and the Double Chocolate Cake Donut, which carries 310 calories and has the texture of igneous rock. But over the past five years, Dunkin' Donuts has sought to reinvent itself as an upstairs-downstairs coffee house. It wants to lure more white-collar customers while tending to its loyal base of proles. As its chief executive officer, Jack Shafer, boasted in 1998, "Our average customer would be as likely to pull up in a BMW or Lexus as they would be to pull up in a pickup truck or on foot."

The middlebrowing of Dunkin' Donuts reverses a half-century of blue-collar bona fides. For years, Dunkin' Donuts embodied the working-class ethos of its founder, Bill Rosenberg, who was raised in Boston's Dorchester neighborhood during the Great Depression. Rosenberg had a reputation as a hustler and street fighter. He had little use for a formal education—he dropped out of school in the eighth grade—but was wont to have dreamy reveries over baked pastry. His 2001 memoir, *Time to Make the Donuts*, is testament to the doughnut's inebriating power. "Boy, those big jelly donuts, yeast raised with granulated sugar on the outside, were so loaded with jelly that when we took a bite out of one, it would squirt. It was fantastic!" (Rosenberg got the idea to write his memoirs from Mario Puzo, whom he met at a weight-loss clinic.)

Rosenberg brought fire and entrepreneurship to Dunkin' Donuts, which he founded in Quincy, Mass., in 1950. Having peddled snacks to factory workers during World War II, he knew how to draw in the proletariat. His coffee was hot and served in seconds; he offered 52 varieties of doughnuts, dozens more than his competitors. An early storefront was situated across the street from a Ford assembly plant in Somerville, Mass., guaranteeing him hundreds of loyal rivet-heads. When Rosenberg began granting franchise licenses a few years later, he hewed to the blue-collar wards of New England and the mid-Atlantic, which had built-in constituencies; even in early 2005, only 70 of the chain's more than 4,000 American outlets were west of the Mississippi.

Like all corporate behemoths, Dunkin' Donuts is a clever thief. The chain waits for other restaurants to innovate, a company vice president told *Business Week Online*, and then "Dunkinizes" the new products. Rosenberg himself pinched the idea for his "52 flavors of donuts" from Howard Johnson's 28 flavors of ice cream. When Einstein's and other bagel houses rallied in the mid-1990s, Dunkin' Donuts put bagels in its glass cases; within a year, it was the No. 1 bagel-seller in America.

But the looming specter of Starbucks—and Rosenberg's retirement in 1988—heralded a new era for the doughnut house. Piece by piece, Dunkin' Donuts began to shed its blue-collar trappings. An early company icon, Fred the Baker—who tirelessly rose in the wee hours and declared, "Time to make the doughnuts"—was pink-slipped in 1997. The 50-year-old "dunkin' donut," which came with a handle for dipping in coffee and was itself an emblem of proletariat manners, had disappeared from most stores by 2003. Meanwhile, to its array of coffee and doughnuts, Dunkin' Donuts added a wide-ranging "espresso platform" and a Frappuccino knock-off called the Coolatta.

Contra Starbucks, Dunkin' Donuts peddles a more populist tone: high-quality coffees without the cultural pretension. A 1998 Dunkin' Donuts commercial featured a prissy Starbucks-style barista, clad in green apron, mocking customers; the ad said that Dunkin' Donuts peddled "a rich, bold blend without all the bitterness." When Dunkin' Donuts found itself challenged by Krispy Kreme, it responded by emphasizing its healthier items and beefing up its espresso menu. Krispy Kreme, once a hot Wall Street stock, was bleeding money by 2004.

In the age of the Atkins diet and the film *Super Size Me*, fast food has become a dicey business. If the late-1990s were about indulgence—Krispy Kreme, the Triple Whopper—then the new century requires a novel approach. Hulking globs of grease are out. But they haven't been replaced by healthier fast food. They have been replaced by what one might call aspirant fast food: hulking globs of grease that want to be something. This is perhaps what prompted Dunkin' Donuts to create the Whole Wheat Donut, which sounds benign but contains a whopping 19 grams of fat. Or to suggest, as one former Dunkin' executive did, that the product's most crucial ingredient isn't enriched flour or partially hydrogenated soybean oil but . . . love: "Customers most commonly associate 'love' with our coffee and doughnuts, ice cream and sandwiches."

Even as Dunkin' Donuts goes upscale, it still has a nagging problem: atmosphere. Whereas Starbucks channels the ambiance of the European coffee bar and Krispy Kreme the sleekness of the '50s diner, Dunkin' Donuts stores have all the warmth of a sanitarium—and, well, an unsanitary one, at that. The color scheme has a high concentration of magenta. (A remodeling plan succeeded only in changing the name of the magenta to "ripe raisin.") Whereas Starbucks and Krispy Kreme invite customers to stay a while, Dunkin' Donuts chases them out the door, as if clinging to the '50s blue-collar ethos of "Back to the plant!"

This approach has made Dunkin' Donuts America's most aloof fast-food franchise. One could argue that doughnuts are meant to be a solitary pleasure, consumed furtively and silently. But must every Dunkin' outlet feature people sitting alone and staring blankly into the industrial lighting? I camped out in the crowded Times Square hub in Manhattan for nearly 30 minutes one afternoon before I heard a grunt that approximated human speech: a man asking another if he could share his table. The seated man replied, "You gotta give me half the stuff on your tray." That just won't do. Dunkin' Donuts can't hope to fend off Starbucks without appropriating some of its talky atmosphere. It's time to make the doughnuts. But first, it's time to make conversation.

Nevada

America's Yucca Mountain of vice.

BY CHRIS SUELLENTROP

IN THE NOVEL *INFINITE JEST,* David Foster Wallace imagines a future America in which a vast swath of the country has been transformed into a repository for the nation's pollution. Giant fans are erected along the border to blow the waste away from the rest of the now-pristine nation. In this future, Americans call this place "The Concavity." In the present, we call it Nevada.

Americans have long thought of Nevada as the place to store our filth, our refuse, our somewhat embarrassing excess. The Senate confirmed this instinct when it voted to ship tens of thousands of tons of nuclear waste to Yucca Mountain, near Mercury, Nev., beginning in 2010. But the phenomenon is cultural as well as physical: Nevada has always been fenced off from the rest of the country as the landfill for our vice, our cultural pollution. It's the place to store the things we want, even need, but must confine: prostitution, mobsters, secret government areas for military testing, and God knows what else. Things we hate to love have been stored there for easy recall: boxing, gambling, Sammy Davis Jr. "The government has always regarded Nevada as a place unlike others, fit for tests, experiments, and ventures it would sometimes rather not talk about," David Thomson writes in *In Nevada: The Land, the People, God, and Chance*.

But it's not just the government or the outsiders that think of Nevada as an experiment. Nevadans themselves think of their state that way, too. If states are the laboratories of democracy, Nevada is the one we've handed over to the mad scientists.

Perhaps it's in their blood. The first Americans to settle in Nevada were themselves unwanted exports, exiles—Mormons shipped west by an uncaring public. The Utah Territory established for Mormon settlers by Congress in 1850 included nearly all of present-day Nevada. Las Vegas, before it was a glorious Technicolor playland, was a Mormon colony (unsurprisingly, a failed one). These Mormons were Nevada's first of many encounters with the national policy of YINBY—Yes, In Nevada's Backyard.

This sense of Nevada as a dumping ground for the country's castoffs continued into the 20th century. The nation nodded approvingly as organized crime flocked to Nevada during the three decades after the state legalized gambling in 1931 (or rather, re-legalized it after a two-decade prohibition). Mormons and mobsters don't have a lot in common, but the thought process was the same: Good riddance. At least they're not here.

And in what other state would Harry Truman have cordoned off a chunk of land the size of Connecticut for nuclear tests and top-secret government research? To this day, the federal government owns 85 percent of the land in Nevada. It's partly because of this (because Nevada is the storehouse of our nation's secrets) that it's easy for some to believe that an alien spaceship landed in Roswell, N.M., and was shipped to Nevada's mysterious Area 51. Nevada would be the obvious choice for something the government wanted to dispose of: Just stick it in the attic and hope everyone forgets about it.

The famous Nevadan distaste for government stems in part from this kind of federal meddling, real and imagined. Nevada's state government itself arrived as an imposition from Uncle Sam. The state came into existence because Lincoln wanted an extra state, to get votes both for his re-election and for the 13th Amendment, outlawing slavery. The fact that Nevada didn't contain enough people to qualify for statehood was conveniently overlooked. That dubious admission to the Union has fostered a still-prevalent local myth in Nevada that Lincoln and the Republicans needed the state's mineral deposits to finance the Civil War.

While Nevada disdains the outsiders who view it as a moral wasteland, it also encourages the perception. The state's economy is fueled by Nevada's special role—it's the place you go to get what you can't get at home. So, when Nevada's vice seeps back out into the rest of the country, Nevada suffers. That's what happened to Reno, which made its name in the 1920s as the divorce capital of the nation. Other states made divorce onerous, but Nevada made it easy. Just live there for six months and you could chuck your spouse overboard. Famous and wealthy men and women flocked to the state. "Divorce ranches" popped up to care for them during their stay. But as the moral stigma of divorce faded, other parts of the country started loosening their requirements, too. Nevada engaged in a race to the bottom, lowering its residency requirement to three months, then six weeks. By the 1960s, Americans didn't need to go to Nevada for divorce. They could get it at home.

Now, something similar may be happening with gambling. Who needs Nevada when you can gamble in Boonville, Mo.; in Sioux City, Iowa; in Peoria, Ill.? Perhaps that fear is behind Nevada's newest experiment, one that hasn't yet passed: the legalization of marijuana possession. A 2002 attempt to legalize possession of up to three ounces was scuttled by voters, but Nevadan lawmakers aren't giving up. They rewrote the petition and are going to try again. Under the proposal, Nevada would tax marijuana and sell it in state-licensed shops. The vices change, but Nevada remains the same.

If marijuana possession becomes legal in the state, many will condemn Nevada for its hedonism, for its willy-nilly disregard for the consequences of its actions. But Nevada knows exactly what it's doing. And so do we. After all, look who's behind the marijuana initiative: the Marijuana Policy Project, an advocacy group based in—where else?—Washington, D.C.

PESTS

August

Let's get rid of it.

BY DAVID PLOTZ

AUGUST IS THE MISSISSIPPI of the calendar. It's beastly hot and muggy. It has a dismal history. Nothing good ever happens in it. And the United States would be better off without it.

August is when the atomic bombs dropped on Hiroshima and Nagasaki, when Anne Frank was arrested, when the first income tax was collected, when Katrina hit New Orleans, when Elvis Presley and Marilyn Monroe died. Wings and Jefferson Airplane were formed in August. *The Sonny and Cher Comedy Hour* debuted in August. (No August, no Sonny and Cher!)

August is the time when thugs and dictators think they can get away with it. World War I started in August 1914. The Nazis and Soviets signed their nonaggression pact in August 1939. Iraq invaded Kuwait on Aug. 2, 1990. August is a popular month for coups and violent crime. Why August? Perhaps the villains assume we'll be too distracted by vacations or humidity to notice.

August is the vast sandy wasteland of American culture. Publishers stop releasing books. Movie theaters are clogged with the egregious action movies that studios wouldn't dare release in June. Television is all reruns. The sports pages wither into nothingness. Pre-pennant-race baseball—if that can even be called a sport—is all that remains. We have to feign interest in NFL training camps. Newspapers are thin in August, but not thin enough. They still print ghastly vacation columns: David Broder musing on world peace from his summer home on Lake Michigan? Even Martha Stewart (born Aug. 3) can't think of anything to do in August. Her *Martha Stewart Living* calendar, usually so sprightly, overflows with ennui. Aug. 14: "If it rains, organize basement." Aug. 16: "Re-seed bare patches in lawn." Aug. 27: "Change batteries in smoke and heat detectors."

You can't get a day off from August, because it is the only month without a real holiday. Instead, the other months have shunted onto this weak sister all the lame celebrations they didn't want. Air Conditioning Appreciation Week, Certified Registered Nurse Anesthetist Week, National Religious Software Week, Carpenter Ant Awareness Week: All these grand American celebrations belong to August. Is it any accident that National Lazy Day, Relaxation Day, Deadwood Day, and Failures Day are commemorated in August?

August is the month of vagueness. October is the 10th month, March is the third month. What's August—bet you can't remember. Does it have 30 days or 31? You have to recite the rhyme to figure that one out. The great writers of history forget August: It rates three mentions in *Bartlett's Quotations*, compared with a dozen for December and two dozen for March.

The people with August birthdays are a sorry bunch. Sure, Lyndon Johnson and Bill Clinton were born in August, but the other presidential Augustans are Herbert Hoover and Benjamin Harrison. Film is represented by Robert Redford and Robert De Niro—but also by John Holmes and Harry Reems. Third-raters populate August: George Hamilton, Danny Bonaduce, Rick Springfield, and Frank and Kathie Lee Gifford were born then. August gave us Fidel Castro and Yasser Arafat. In art, August offers Leni Riefenstahl, Michael Jackson, and Danielle Steele. (To be sure, not everything that happens in August is so terrible. Raoul Wallenberg, Alfred Hitchcock, Herman Melville, and Mae West were born in August. Richard Nixon resigned in August. MTV launched in August. And Jerry Garcia died in August.)

August can't even master the things it is supposed to do well. Despite its slothful reputation, it is not the top vacation month, July is. Nor is August the hottest month (on the East Coast, at least). That crown, too, is July's. August is when the garden starts to wither, and when the long summer days cruelly vanish.

We should rage, rage against the dying of the light. The United States desperately needs August Reform. Purists will insist that we shouldn't tinker with the months, that August should be left alone because it has done workmanlike service for 2,000 years. That's nonsense. Calendars are always fluxing. August itself was a whimsical invention. In 46 B.C., as part of a broad calendar change, Julius Caesar added two days to Sextilis, an old 29-day month. In the reign of his successor, Augustus Caesar, the Senate voted to change Sextilis' name to "Augustus" (as the Senate under Julius Caesar had renamed the month before, "Quintilis," "Julius").

August was created by politics, and it can be undone by politics. For too long, bureaucrats in Washington have been telling you how you must divide up your calendar. But these are your months, and you should be able to do with them what you like. Genuine August Reform will be hard. It will require tough compromises to protect the special interests of September and July. (And who better to sponsor this revolution, incidentally, than Sen. John McCain—birthday Aug. 29?)

Here is a framework for compromise. Cede the first 10 days of August back to July, thus extending holiday revelry for more than a week. September would claim the last 10 days of August, mollifying the folks who can't wait to get back to serious work. Labor Day would come 10 days earlier, the school year would run longer, and the rush of fall activity could get jump-started. August itself will keep 10 days. That is just enough: Every summer we'll be able to toot happily, "Gosh, August went by so quickly this year!"

And as for the 31st day, it will be designated a holiday independent from any month. It will fall after the 10th and last day of August, and it will celebrate the end of that most useless month.

The Dalai Lama

The ambassador from Shangri-La sells the romance of Tibet. The West is buying.

BY DAVID PLOTZ

2006—IT'S THE "YEAR OF TIBET" AGAIN, this time in Australia and New Zealand. It was France's turn to celebrate the "Year of Tibet" in 2005. Before that, Hollywood honored the Land of Snows with its 1997 "Year of Tibet in Movies." The press proclaimed the "Year of Tibet" when the Dalai Lama won the Nobel Peace Prize in 1989. America and Europe feted an "International Year of Tibet" two years later. At the center of the adulation is, of course, the Dalai Lama, who at this very moment is almost certainly making yet another triumphal world tour, in which he's being introduced by celebrity Buddhist Richard Gere and treated to the kind of gushy press coverage that other world leaders (and lamas) can only fantasize about.

The Dalai Lama is, by all accounts, a true holy man: humble, devout, warm, funny, as sweet inside as outside. He casts himself as a Himalayan Forrest Gump—the accidental guru: "I am just a simple Buddhist monk." But this humility, which is undoubtedly sincere, also serves the Dalai Lama's shrewd PR campaign. His Holiness is cashing in on the West's romance with Eastern spirituality, using it to attract international sympathy. Dressed in his maroon robes and beatific smile, the Dalai Lama—the Ocean of Wisdom, the Protector of the Land of Snows, the White Lotus—symbolizes all that's right with the East and wrong with the West.

He is the ambassador from Shangri-La, emissary from a magical, peaceful land protected by stunning mountains, dotted with magnificent temples, ruled by wise and benevolent priest-kings.

Nearly 60 years after China conquered Tibet, the Dalai Lama and his long-suffering subjects have achieved a victory of sorts: They have become the world's champion victims. They are, as Buddhist scholar Robert Thurman (father of Uma) once told the *New York Times*, "the baby seals of the human rights movement." Other trampled nations briefly seize the world's attention, then disappear. No movie stars ever demonstrated for Estonian independence. East Timor—yesterday's news. The Afghans and Iraqis are making headlines these days, but it won't last. China overran the Muslim state of East Turkestan the same year it grabbed Tibet: Have you ever heard of it? Tibet's "god-king" is cornering the market in human rights.

A Buddhist theocracy, Tibet was (more or less) independent for thousands of years, mostly because it was so inhospitable to invaders. But in 1950, Mao reasserted an ancient Chinese claim to it, and troops stormed the plateau. The Dalai Lama, who had been chosen for the post as a 4-year-old boy in 1939, cooperated with the Chinese authorities for a while. But in the midst of a failed Tibetan rebellion in 1959, he fled to northern India, where he's lived ever since. In the meantime, the occupying Chinese army murdered hundreds of thousands of Tibetan civilians. Hundreds of thousands more starved during a famine caused by demented Chinese agricultural policy. The Chinese tried to obliterate Buddhist culture: Celibate nuns and priests were forced to copulate in the street; others were crucified or dragged to death by horses. All but 13 of Tibet's 6,000-plus monasteries were looted and ransacked. Officially, Tibet is an "Autonomous Region." In fact, China controls its government, economy, and education.

The Dalai Lama's only tool is moral suasion. He wields it magnificently. He feeds his Western audiences a softhearted, softheaded universalism, a religion without dogma, an Ansel Adams photograph. He bathes his U.S. audiences in kindly aphorisms: "Be a nice person. Be a good person." "Happiness produces health. Medical scientists accept this." "We should learn together as brothers and sisters in the great human family." (We should.) We should also: protect the environment, forgive those who abuse us, know that satisfaction does not come from material things, and escape from hustle and bustle. The Dalai Lama's pop Buddhism is appealingly self-centered: Happiness trumps everything. This is a winning idea in our therapeutic culture: a religion that's about my satisfaction, not God's.

The Dalai Lama keeps the message cheerful. Who needs some gloomy Gus who harangues you about torture, rape, and murder all the time? The Dalai Lama is the Fun Prophet. He laughs. He tells jokes—mostly at his own expense. He even guest-edited an issue of *Vogue*. He pronounces himself "always optimistic" (though if there's any person whom history should have taught not to be optimistic, surely it's the Dalai Lama).

Americans and Europeans, especially those susceptible to New Age spirituality, find his mixture of exoticism, aphorism, and optimism irresistible. *Kundun* and *Seven Years in Tibet* presented the Dalai Lama's autobiography as hagiography. Harrison Ford bore witness at congressional hearings. The Beastie Boys, Smashing Pumpkins, and R.E.M. have headlinined benefit concerts with Tibetan performers in New York and San Francisco.

In recent years, the Dalai Lama's roster of tangible accomplishments has been negligible. The Chinese government refuses to negotiate with him. The crackdown on Tibetan religion has not improved. In 1995, after the Dalai Lama chose a 6-year-old boy to be Panchen Lama, Tibet's second-most powerful religious leader, the Chinese kidnapped him and installed another 6-year-old boy. The original Panchen Lama is still missing, presumably under house arrest somewhere in China.

In a way, the Dalai Lama may reinforce Chinese authority over Tibet. He insists that Tibetans abjure violence, threatening to abdicate if Tibetans take arms against the Chinese. But non-violent resistance tends to succeed when 1) the world is watching and 2) the oppressors care. The Chinese seem indifferent, and the world will only pay attention as long as the Dalai Lama is alive. (Many observers believe the Chinese won't negotiate with the elderly lama because they are holding out for his death. At that point, the outside pressure for a peaceful accommodation will vanish.) Among Tibetans, frustration with the Dalai Lama's placid pacifism has grown. Saints never exhaust their patience, but sometimes their followers do. Soon it will be too late for Tibetans, if it isn't already. Thanks to Chinese migration policies, Tibet now has more Han Chinese than Tibetans. Soon the Dalai Lama's Tibet will be a Shangri-La in another way: merely a memory of a land that has been destroyed by outsiders.

Big-Screen Televisions

A moral dilemma.

BY BRYAN CURTIS

BEFORE WE CONFRONT the moral dilemma posed by big-screen televisions, a quick story. A revelation, really. Scene: Sunday night in January. Location: Bar. Occasion: NFL playoffs. Alcohol: Yes.

I'm prattling on about some football star I know nothing about when I glance at the bar's big-screen TV and notice something marvelous: linemen's breath. The network was locked on one of those "eye-of-God" shots, the camera hovering a few hundred feet above the players. But with the clarity of the plasma TV, you could see the individual breaths of defensive linemen escaping from their face masks into the cold air. Perhaps it was the Amstel Light, but I was moved. I reached a similar high a few months later, when the *New York Times* reported that manufacturers like Panasonic were on the brink of a murderous price war, which will drive big-screens into range for those of us not pulling down NFL salaries. Tons of late adopters seemed poised, like me, to buy their first televisual behemoth, conveniently forgetting the days when the big-screen TV seemed, you know, sort of uncouth. So remind me again: Why did we decide it was OK to admit hulking, 65-inch black boxes into our living rooms?

Falling prices, rising quality—yes. But there's more to it. Like the Gap T-shirt or *Maxim*, a big-screen TV carries its own set of social implications. The first big-screens with a quality picture were turned out by Mitsubishi in the late 1970s and peddled by retailers like Southern California's Paul Goldenberg, the self-proclaimed "King of Big Screen." In the early days, Goldenberg and his cohorts catered mostly to niche markets: the super-rich (for whom the big-screen was merely another fob) and lonely cinephiles and sports fanatics (for whom the big-screen was a beloved friend). On the other side of the spectrum, rent-to-own shops "leased" big-screen TVs to the creditless for 185 percent of their value. It wasn't until two decades later, during the free-wheeling Clintonian 1990s, that the big-screen began to really catch on with the middle class—in part because of early price wars, and in part because of a burst of competitive spending that also fueled the heyday of the SUV and McMansion. In 1994, *Consumer Electronics* reported that big-screen TVs were outselling their midsize counterparts for the first time in history.

The first dilemma posed by the big-screen is where to put the thing. Just how comfortable you are introducing a big-screen into your home might depend (to cop a line from the former president) on what your definition of "living room" is. The big-screen is a black hole of design. Admitting one into your living room will suck the life force from your leather sectional, fireplace, and Pre-Raphaelite art pieces. Pair the big-screen with a stereo and the cumulative effect is to morph the living room into an "entertainment room," in which the gadgetry dictates the ambience. Bright colors and rich leathers give way to razor-sharp black edges. In 1995, the *Los Angeles Times* reported that new-home builders had begun to reconfigure rooms around the big-screen—which the paper referred to, brightly, as the "new hearth."

This is different than the old axiom about the TV taking over the house. Here the problem isn't whether to pledge your devotion to Uncle Television; it's whether he should be allowed to move in and remodel. Where small TVs can be concealed in an armoire, in most cases a big-screen must remain alfresco. The solution for some families has been to embrace the big-screen as an art object. This, too, conforms to a new ideal of the American household. As the population drifts toward the exurbs, small flourishes make otherwise identical houses stand out. "When you live in the land of McMansions, you want to adorn your house to create some sense of difference," says Kevin Delaney, a sociologist at Temple University. "And having the latest TV on the wall is one of the ways to do it." Honey, who are the Moores again? Those nice people down the block, with the two young girls and the 65-inch Mitsubishi Medallion.

It follows that rich and poor viewers alike would dream about upgrading to 72-inch glory. For this reason, the big-screen has become a useful tool in amateur class theorizing. That is, the big-screen can symbolize virtually anything you want about any social class. In the case of the middle class, for example, the big-screen is often derided as a risible symbol of overconsumption—another totem to keep up with the Joneses. ("It frightens me to be sensitive to the idea that my neighbor just got a big-screen TV that's three inches bigger than mine," a banker told *Fortune* in 1987. "But that's something I look at.") A brighter view holds that the big-screen TV is a democratizing cultural force. It has turned us all into movie connoisseurs—allowing us to finally appreciate widescreen DVDs and surround sound in our "home theaters." Robert Thompson, a historian at Syracuse University, contends that the near-cinematic artistry of HBO shows like *The Sopranos* and *Carnivále* is due, in part, to improving technology. "The producers want to make sure these things have equity value built up," Thompson says. "So when we're watching *The Sopranos* in reruns ten years from now, on a big-screen, it will still look good."

The working poor also have a tenuous relationship with the big-screen. Conservative critics might see the presence of a big-screen in a dilapidated tract house as a product of misguided spending; for liberals, it could merely represent inchoate class longings. In a heartbreaking example that would satisfy both camps, the *Los Angeles Times* profiled a family of four—total household income: $19,000—who had driven themselves to the brink of insolvency by buying a big-screen TV. In 1998, a *Business Week* writer described his amazement upon entering the house of a down-at-the-heels Massachusetts woman: "I beheld the trappings of upper-middle-class comfort. The big-screen TV and VCR. The crush of name-brand toys. And outside, the fairly new Lincoln Town Car—for which she was several months behind on payments."

Such tales shouldn't tamp down our big-screen lust. If we're all trashing our living rooms (and our credit ratings) for the latest bourgeois trapping, then at least we're doing it together. Call me uncultivated and aesthetically dense; call me a vile social climber; call me an adherent of the "new hearth"—but I want to see linemen's breath, and I want it now.

Jane Fonda

What does she want from us?

BY BRYAN CURTIS

THOSE WHO THINK JANE FONDA'S sole raison d'être is to annoy conservative opinion writers should note this passage from her memoir, *My Life So Far*. The year is 1970. Fonda has just engaged in her very first acts of civil disobedience, on behalf of aggrieved Native American tribes. The protests, she writes, "morphed me from a noun to a verb. A verb is active and less ego-oriented. Being a verb means being defined by action, not by title." So there. Jane Fonda aspired to something greater than husband-swapping and liberal do-gooding; she wanted to become a part of speech. Fonda (*v.*): to plead for social justice until humanity can't take it anymore.

My Life So Far heralded the emergence of a new Fonda—what she called her "Phoenix," poised to lift off from Atlanta at any moment. This follows on the heels of at least four previous permutations of Fonda: the *Barbarella* sex goddess, the lefty, the aerobics instructor, and, more recently, the tireless Braves fan. So what is this new Fonda like? Savvier than "Hanoi Jane," for sure, but slightly frailer than the aerobics queen—she faced hip-replacement surgery at the conclusion of the book tour. Previous incarnations of Fonda wanted our hearts, our minds, our abdominals. What does this new Fonda want from us?

Plainly, not our forgiveness. In the preface of her book, Fonda announced her intention to "set the record straight" about her 1972 adventure in North Vietnam, which remains potent ammunition for the right. (See, for example, the forged photograph of Fonda and John Kerry that turned up during the 2004 presidential campaign.) But Fonda offered little new about Vietnam and even fewer words of contrition—and these only for posing in front of an anti-aircraft gun, which she says she wandered in front of by mistake. "I carry this heavy in my heart," she writes, an apology that will satisfy no one, least of all the neocon grunts who regularly emerge to denounce her on *The O'Reilly Factor*. The one revelation she offers? That she determined to have a second child after spotting a female North Vietnamese soldier who was manning a gun installation while pregnant.

Nor does Fonda, as she limps into her eighth decade, have much desire to entertain. *My Life So Far* swelled to 579 uninspiring pages. If one suspected that Hollywood memoirs emerge as a byproduct of therapy sessions, Fonda removed all doubt, importing a team of shrinks to elucidate key moments in her life: "Dr. Blumenthal told me that Mother's behavior suggests that she may have been suffering from post-partum depression. . . ." Only rarely would Fonda unleash the charm-bombs that made her the most winsome actress of the 1970s. She playfully growled at rival diva Faye Dunaway and dropped a few Hollywood anecdotes: "[T]here was a loud noise, some plaster fell from the ceiling, and an owl fell onto Gore Vidal's plate."

What Fonda wants, it seems, is a messy public divorce from the men in her life. She says her ever-mutating public image was stage-managed by men, who sought to mold her in their own image. Most fearsome was her late father, Henry, who treated her and her brother Peter like a pair of particularly unloved pets. Henry Fonda was a cold, churlish man; he is said to have cried only once, upon learning of the death of Franklin Roosevelt. His aloofness drove Fonda's mother, Frances, into a sanitarium, where she committed suicide by cutting her throat. (Fonda, then in grade school, learned the news by reading a film magazine.) Henry drifted in and out of Fonda's life, occasionally reappearing to upbraid her for her nascent activism. It left Jane perplexed: How could the man who played Abraham Lincoln, Tom Joad, and Clarence Darrow turn a cold eye to social justice?

Fonda's three husbands proved even more loathsome. She flitted from director Roger Vadim to lefty rabblerouser Tom Hayden to Ted Turner, perhaps the only man on the planet whose liberal do-gooding is more schizophrenic than her own. Their union was like the merger of two giant charities. Turner called Fonda the day after her divorce from Hayden hits the newspapers to ask her out on a date. She demurred. He called back three months later, and she accepted. She appeared in a black miniskirt, halter top, and spike heels, and Turner becomes so excited that he has to excuse himself six times during dinner to use the toilet. On their second date, at Turner's Montana ranch, the billionaire pleaded, "Come on, why don't we make love? Huh?" When Fonda relented, Turner squealed, "Hot dog!" Fonda would say little about the aerobics that followed, though she coyly alluded to the spurting fountains of Versailles. After nine years of marriage, Turner dumped Fonda for what he charmingly referred to as his "backup."

Fonda has suggested that you can trace each personality to a particular husband. Vadim, a pal of Albert Camus and Henry Miller who preferred his leading ladies to perform in zero-gravity, molded her into a vapid sex goddess. Hayden turned her to liberal martyrdom and, later, when his charities needed infusions of cash, aerobics. Turner, the most domineering of the three, abhorred Fonda's acting and freelance activism. He wanted a trophy wife and someone to sit with at day games—hence Fonda's decade-long exile in Atlanta.

The rule-of-man theory tied *My Life So Far* together in a neat, therapeutic kind of way, but you ultimately feel that Fonda is playing a bit coy with us. Roger Vadim is dead and largely forgotten; Hayden and Turner's liberal empires have withered. And yet when Fonda goes on *60 Minutes,* it stirs up more caterwauling and demagoguery than anything since the appearance of the Swift Boat

Veterans for Truth. Perhaps Fonda is so mired in new-age body talk—"my daughter's home had become a womb in which I was pregnant with myself"—that she cannot see that she has outdistanced her former keepers. If "fonda" has indeed become a verb, perhaps what it means is to sell oneself short.

Michael Crichton

Planet Earth's novelist of doom.

BY BRYAN CURTIS

THE OFFICIAL TITLE OF PULP WRITER to the White House has passed to Michael Crichton. What Tom Clancy was for Ronald Reagan, and Joe Klein was for Bill Clinton, Crichton has become for George W. Bush, who recently invited the novelist over for an hour-long chat. The subject was Crichton's views on global warming, as he'd expounded upon in his novel *State of Fear*. After the discussion, the journalist Fred Barnes reported, Crichton and Bush found themselves in "near-total agreement." Months earlier, the novelist had testified before a Senate committee on climate change, raising more dire warnings. It is a perch perfect for Crichton, Planet Earth's novelist of doom.

Crichton's *State of Fear* is a 600-page novel about global warming, an op-ed posing as pulp fiction. Crichton thinks environmentalists have become overheated about the threat of climate change and have substituted demagoguery for hard science. So in the book his villains are a cabal of evil greens, who build weather machines to punish their SUV-drivin', carbon-dioxide-emittin' neighbors. There might be *American Enterprise* fellows who jumped at this news, but for us Crichton fans this was close to heartbreaking. The boy-novelist who engineered a tyrannosaurus in *Jurassic Park,* mysterious pathogens from outer space in *The Andromeda Strain*, and killer gorillas in *Congo,* has become a political pamphleteer, a right-wing noodge.

In some ways, Crichton's pedant period was inevitable. His prose was always curiously formal for a thriller writer. He wrote about childlike subjects in a fussy, professorial way—his tyrannosaurus was not a fearsome mass of skin and teeth (as Ray Bradbury had it) but the sum of its DNA. It wasn't just the hard science, either. Crichton described his human characters as a field biologist describes a giraffe: "He was surprisingly tall, maybe a hundred and ninety centimeters, well over six feet." Crichton's adventurers were invariably white men with advanced degrees—paleontologists, psychologists, lawyers. Like the biology professors in Arthur Conan Doyle's *The Lost World*, Crichton devoted his books to the notion that gentlemen-scholars can venture into the wild and, between claps of machine-gun fire, discuss the latest articles from the scientific journals.

Crichton was himself as a 20th-century Renaissance man, a dabbler in all the fine arts and sciences. After graduating from medical school at Harvard, he became, at various turns, a novelist, film director (*Westworld*, *Coma*), screenwriter (*Jurassic Park*), TV series creator (*ER*), futurist, and author of a competent monograph about Jasper Johns. Success came fast and easy. In *Travels*, his 1988 memoir, he wrote about his first midlife crisis: "I had gradated from Harvard, taught at Cambridge University, climbed the Great Pyramid, earned a medical degree, married and divorced, been a postdoctoral fellow at the Salk Institute, published two bestselling novels, and now made a movie. And I had abruptly run out of goals for myself." Crichton was 30 years old.

Crichton has always eschewed flesh-and-blood heroes; the star of his book is usually a high-concept premise—dinosaurs! killer viruses! sexual harassment! Crichton has an unparalleled genius for this—a gift for seeing op-ed-worthy topics years into the future. He began writing *Rising Sun* when the Berlin Wall was crumbling; by the time the book was published, in 1992, George Bush had thrown up in the lap of the Japanese prime minister. Before Bill and Monica hooked up, Crichton published *Disclosure*, a story of sexual harassment in the corridors of power. It was little surprise that the same week *State of Fear* hit bookstores ecoterrorists of the kind Crichton had invented began popping up in the *Washington Times* and other newspapers.

In Crichton's more far-fetched fantasies, the pleasure lies in his erudite polish. You can imagine Crichton leafing through obscure journals and textbooks to find scientific underpinnings for his outlandish premises. (Evidence of Crichton's genius: About half the world still believes you can re-engineer dinosaurs with DNA from mosquitoes.) It feels like an overeducated novelist's penance for writing about the stuff of little boys, and it's reliably charming. But when Crichton begins to proselytize, as he has in recent books, the journal citations and speechifying begins to seem dreary. Instead of being charmed by the nerdy footnotes, you begin to dread them.

This isn't to say that Crichton doesn't believe his right-leaning, contrarian poses—global warming is overstated; etc. Nor is it to say that because the poses are right-leaning that they're invalid or unworthy of somnambulant discussion on the Sunday morning shows. The problem is that any novel based on climate change, Japanese trade policy, or sexual harassment is, with few exceptions, destined to be a complete bore. Crichton's early books were thrillers that, as a side benefit, happened to be instructive. His political books are policy papers that incidentally turn out to be thrillers. Crichton's early work seemed to be conceived on a kind of authorial dare—How can I convince people that dinosaurs could exist in the real world? But as Crichton waded into the real world, and the documentary elements have become the backbone, his charm has disappeared.

Lately, Crichton has felt like a college professor who insists on lecturing 10 minutes after the class period ends. In *State of Fear*, the thriller stops cold for pages and pages of climate graphs ("Goteborg, Sweden: 1951–2004"). When one of Crichton's heroic skeptics makes a statement about global warming, Crichton tags it with a footnote, which have never been the friend of a pulp novelist.

State of Fear ends with 20 pages of bibliographical references and the author's 25-point "message" about global warming. It's a bulwark for what Crichton anticipated would be a backlash from the newspapers, the same sour reaction that greeted *Rising Sun* and *Disclosure*. (George F. Will was a fan of the latter book, but that proves the point.) That's all well and good, but doesn't somebody actually have to finish reading *State of Fear*?

There are moments when Crichton seems to sense that he's become too much of a pedant. As *State of Fear* stumbles to a close, he wedges in some swashbuckling pratfalls that would have impressed Doyle and H. Rider Haggard. The heroes are kidnapped by cannibals in the Solomon Islands, who tie them to wooden posts and poke at them with bats and knives. At another moment, a woman fleeing from a man-made lightning storm—don't ask—crawls smack-dab into the middle of a nest of . . . scorpions! Why scorpions? I haven't a clue. But I loved it. It's like something a grade-schooler would have dreamed up—it has childlike, "top this" passion. Amid the pages of climate charts, the kind of thrills fit for a congressional committee hearing, it may be the only proof Michael Crichton hasn't become a dinosaur.

Jenna and Barbara Bush

The party girls reconsidered.

BY MICHAEL CROWLEY

FROM THE EARLIEST DAYS of the republic, American presidents have been humiliated by their wayward and self-destructive children. John Quincy Adams' son was a debt-laden alcoholic who was kicked out of Harvard and later drowned in a possible suicide. Andrew Jackson Jr. was a decadent freeloader whose mother was once shocked to discover his collection of "disgusting pictures of nature." William Henry Harrison referred to his incompetent sons as "the destruction of my hopes" (although his grandson, Benjamin, became president).

Modern presidential kids haven't fared much better. John F. Kennedy Jr. labored all his life to be taken seriously before his untimely death. Amy Carter was known as a spoiled brat and later flunked out of Brown. Reagan daughter Patti Davis took drugs and married a yoga instructor, posed nude for *Playboy*, and penned erotic novels with names such as *Bondage*. And while George W. Bush has (for better or worse) matched his dad's success, it took him almost 20 years to realize that college was over.

These cases aren't flukes. "Being related to a president [brings] more problems than opportunities," explains Doug Wead, a former aide to George W. Bush, in his book *All the President's Children*. Wead's historical research, he writes, found "higher than average rates of divorce and alcoholism and even premature death. Some presidential children seemed bent on self-destruction." Wead theorizes, a bit crudely, that the pressure to win the approval of a father who also happens to be a world leader simply crushes many presidential offspring.

By these standards Bush's twin daughters, who, after graduating from college in 2004 and finally revealing themselves to the public during the presidential campaign, almost look like overachievers. Yes, they come across as obnoxious, pampered party girls—stylish vixens straight out of *Rich Girls* or *The Simple Life*. Tales may abound of their bad manners, including casual obnoxiousness toward their Secret Service details. And though they keep gossip columnists and paparazzi busy, they seem strangely uninterested in the world around them. But if the Bush girls can manage to stay alive and sane—or at least out of *Playboy*—they'll be in comparatively good shape.

Jenna and Barbara are fraternal twins, delivered within a minute of each other by Caesarian section on Nov. 25, 1981. (According to Ronald Kessler's new authorized biography of the first lady, *Laura Bush: An Intimate Portrait of the First Lady*, the twins owe their conception to fertility drugs. Laura only became pregnant with the twins after beginning a regime of clomiphene citrate, which stimulates ovulation and increases the production of eggs, often resulting in multiple births.) They're far from identical. Like the Bush family itself, there's a cultural duality to them. The first President Bush was the blueblood son of a Connecticut senator who summered in Kennebunkport, Maine. George W. also attended Andover and Yale but remade himself from preppy scion into a boots-wearin' oilman; now he summers in Crawford, Texas, and seems far more Houston than Greenwich. The twins have split this difference. Jenna is the Red Stater: She stayed at home in Austin to attend the University of Texas. "I knew I wanted to go to a big Southern school," she told *Vogue*. Barbara channels the family's Eastern-elite spirit. She applied to nine colleges, including Princeton and Harvard, wound up at Yale, and made regular trips from New Haven into Manhattan. The split also reflects the differences between their parents. Jenna emulates her father's mischievous spirit, while Barbara seems to have inherited more of her mother's bookish reserve.

What they do share is a taste for hip clothes, a good party, and a celebrity milieu (they've reportedly clinked glasses with P. Diddy and Ashton Kutcher). OK, so they're not a couple of Chelsea Clintons. But in historical terms—and especially given what we know about their dad's own reckless youth—they could be a lot worse. That may be partly because George and Laura have been more libertarian than conservative in their parenting. As the *Washington Post*'s Ann Gerhart details in her biography of Laura Bush, *The Perfect Wife*, the Bushes have been permissive, laissez-faire parents more interested in shielding their daughters from prying eyes than in drumming solid values into them. Fearing that media scrutiny could warp their girls, the Bushes fiercely hid them from the public throughout W.'s career. Until the summer of 2004, Bush never brought his daughters on the campaign trail or included them in official family portraits. (Although it's not quite true that they were never used for photo-ops. "George [H.W.] came out after our little talk and was immediately rushed by the grandchildren—as primed by the handlers," Barbara Bush the grandmother once wrote in her diary.) After Bush's election in 2000, the White House pressured national reporters to leave the girls alone—even bullying them if necessary. After one scribe asked a question at a White House briefing that referred to Jenna's drinking, press secretary Ari Fleischer called him later to creepily warn that the question had been "noted in the building."

But this zealous privacy strategy was imperfect. Back in Texas, it kept the girls' pictures out of the newspapers. That worked fine when they were younger. But it didn't help them when they decided to rebel. Once they tasted the freedom of college in 2000, the twins reacted with typical undergraduate abandon: binge-drinking, using fake IDs (and, less typical for undergrads, ditching their Secret Service agents). Even then, the news media mostly looked the other way (except in extreme cases, such as to report the girls' run-ins with the police for underage drinking). But there was no controlling the tabloids, which reported lurid tales of public makeout sessions and other alcohol-soaked debauches. And in a world of cell-phone cameras and mass e-mail, every drunken dirty dance or topple from a barstool could be chronicled at sites such as TheFirstTwins.com. (Sample excerpt from one correspondent: "It was an interesting conversation she was having, and I wish I could have gotten a pic of her grabbing her breasts. She seemed to be a very nice person.")

With the girls starting to acquire something of a trashy image—and a dicey re-election campaign coming up—the Bush family realized the media could be their friend after all. Thus began a slick makeover campaign. In summer 2004 the first daughters were unveiled to the world with all the coordinated hype of Apple's latest iPod rollout. First came a *Vogue* magazine spread, featuring the girls in elegant designer gowns, and their first-ever print interview. Then Jenna appeared at some of her father's campaign events, followed soon after by her sister. In July 2004, they even made solo headline appearances at a handful of campaign events and hosted an online chat on the Bush campaign Web site. It's not hard to guess what these campaign moves were about: A president seen as a blustery warmonger can surely use a couple of pretty young daughters by his side to help soften his image. As soon as Bush won the election, the twins again fell out of the limelight. Have they been pushed back into their protective bubble, or has the world simply moved on? Now the twin's shopping sprees and of-age drunken antics at preppy Georgetown bars garners them only brief, infrequent mentions in the *Washington Post* style section.

This strategic roll-out was a bit propagandistic—but, so what? The Bush girls deserve a little good press. They've been held to standards that millions of college students couldn't meet—partly because they are presidential daughters, and partly because they are daughters of this president, and therefore are assumed to have inherited his youthful fecklessness and dipsomania. A prudish media tittered for years over their collegiate drinking exploits. But what could be more ordinary? It's true that they seem strangely uninterested in the exhilarating world history unfolding around them—"I'm just not political. . . . There's nothing about the process that has ever interested me," Jenna said—but there are worse things. They could be robotic drones reciting their dad's good-versus-evil rhetoric from talking points. Or worse, aspiring Manhattan PR girls. Instead, almost two years after their father's re-election, Jenna is gainfully employed teaching second grade at the Elsie Whitlow Stokes Community Freedom Public Charter School in Washington, D.C., while Barbara has spent time volunteering (under a cover of anonymity) in a Red Cross Children's hospital in Capetown, South Africa. And both have shown flashes of political independence: Jenna is reported to have protested her father's 1998 execution of Karla Faye Tucker, while Barbara was recently quoted as telling a friend she doesn't accept the label of "Republican."

It's true that the Bush girls have wealth and privilege on their side. But dark psychological forces are aligned against them. In addition to the unique pressures borne by presidential children, daughters face an especially complex set of expectations involving feminine virtue and intelligence and ambition. Chelsea, for all she's been through, managed to thread this needle. But it's not easy. So, don't be too hard on the Bush girls. The odds are against them.

Dave Pelzer

The child-abuse entrepreneur.

BY DAVID PLOTZ

DAVE PELZER, THE MOST FAMOUS author you've never read, has spent most of the last decade camped out on the *New York Times* nonfiction best-seller list. Pelzer, whose most insistent piece of advice is "don't dwell on the past," dwells on it very profitably. At 46, he has already written a quartet of memoirs. *A Child Called "It": One Child's Courage to Survive* chronicles how his mother tortured him from age 4 to 12. It has sold more than 2 million copies and spent six years on the best-seller lists. Its sequel, *The Lost Boy: A Foster Child's Search for the Love of a Family*, rehashes the maternal abuse and documents his wild teen-age years. It has sold more than a million copies and had four years as a best seller. The third book, *A Man Named Dave: A Story of Triumph and Forgiveness*, recounts his mother's cruelty again and tells how the adult Pelzer learned to cope with the memory of it. It did two years on the list. A fourth memoir, the less gloomy *The Privilege of Youth*, briefly charted in 2004, too.

Pelzer's books come programmed for big sales. They straddle all the trendy genres: confessional memoir, childhood trauma, triumph-over-adversity, and self-help. Pelzer also owes his success to tireless marketing. For years he has crisscrossed the country lecturing on child abuse and boosting *A Child Called "It."* His indefatigable promotion eventually landed him on the *Montel Williams Show*, which rocketed *A Child Called "It"* to fame.

But there is a creepier reason for Pelzermania. He has turned child abuse into entertainment. Pelzer likes to be known as the guy who "makes child abuse fun." He repeatedly refers to himself as "Robin Williams in glasses." His public appearances are manic and joking, filled with imitations of Arnold Schwarzenegger and Bill Clinton. He craves a career in stand-up comedy. (If Schadenfreude is joy at others' sorrow, what is joy at your own?)

Pelzer's books aren't funny, but they do entertain in a darker way. *In Erotic Innocence: The Culture of Child Molesting*, James Kincaid argues that child sexual abuse became a cultural obsession in the '80s in part because the stories of abuse were enthralling, at once erotic and grotesque. Pelzer's memoirs lack sexual abuse—the only kind of savagery that's missing—but they appeal to a similar sense of voyeurism and transgression. *A Child Called "It"* is the most sickeningly violent book I've ever read: It's snuff literature.

As Pelzer tells in *A Child Called "It"*—then retells in the sequels—his sweetness-and-light California family disintegrated in the mid-'60s. His dipso mother—a Mengele of the burbs—inexplicably singled out the 4-year-old for an escalating campaign of torture. Even as she treated his brothers kindly, she ground Dave's face into soiled diapers and made him eat dog shit. She starved him for weeks at a time and made him vomit after school to make sure he wasn't sneaking food. When he tried stealing scraps from the garbage, she laced the trashcan with ammonia. She forced him to take long ice-cold baths and shoved spoonfuls of ammonia down his throat. Often she locked him in the bathroom with a bucket of ammonia and Clorox: The toxic fumes in the "gas chamber" burned his esophagus and nearly killed him. She beat him with a dog chain, a broom, her fists, burned him on the gas stove, stabbed him in the chest, then left him to clean up the wound. She referred to him as "The Boy" and "It." His feckless, drunken father watched in silence, not daring to risk his wife's wrath.

After eight years of this, Pelzer's teachers rescued him and spirited him into foster care. Eventually he managed to join the Air Force, marry, earn a college degree, and straighten out. His mother escaped punishment because, he says, child-abuse laws were weak in the early '70s.

There are no people in Pelzer's book, only demons (his mother and grandmother), angels (Pelzer and a few foster parents), and incompetents. Psychological motivation scarcely interests him. He makes only a halfhearted effort to explain his mother's lunacy. The point is the suffering. As the trilogy progresses, Pelzer is forced to increase the dosage of wickedness to top what came before. (Iron law of sequels: They must be bloodier than the original.) His mother becomes more cartoonish, more Cruella De Vil. In the first book, she's horrible but erratic. By the third she is the incarnation of pure, calculating evil, saying things like, "You gave me no pleasure, so you were disposed of."

Pelzer's dialogue, which is full of such over-the-top lines, is sometimes suspicious. Though it's reconstructed 20 or 30 years after the fact, it is eerily precise. His stories often seem too elaborate, detailed, and graphic to be real—especially since he can't remember any information that might corroborate them. There's no doubt he was horribly abused, and no one has disputed any of his tales, but they are mostly irrefutable. Almost everyone who could question them—including his mother and father—has died. The few who could are skeptical: His grandmother has said the books should be shelved under "fiction." (Like that other memoirist of suffering, James Frey, Pelzer got a big boost from Oprah.) The abuse memoir is a family business with the Pelzers: His brother Richard, who doesn't talk to Dave, wrote his own book in 2005.

Pelzer's fame certainly can't be explained by literary merit. Unlike Mary Karr and Frank McCourt, fellow serial memoirists of terrible childhoods, Pelzer lacks prose ambition. His writing plods. "A single tear" is always rolling down someone's cheek, and he never tires of the "unconquerable human spirit."

Still, Pelzer has other virtues. He really does inspire abuse victims. Online bulletin boards overflow with gratitude from fellow survivors: If he overcame a hellish beginning and made a normal, happy life for himself, then I can too. He relentlessly encourages other troubled kids to be resilient and stop wallowing. He deserves credit for publicizing physical abuse, the déclassé stepsister of sexual molestation. In all the uproar over child sexual abuse, few writers but Pelzer have focused on physical abuse, though it's much more common and often more damaging. Most depictions of childhood trauma paint authority figures as bad-hearted and indifferent. Pelzer, who was rescued by teachers, cops, and social workers and lived with a series of benevolent foster families, honors them. Some teacher-training programs even use Pelzer's book to hearten new teachers about the good they can do.

Pelzer is magnificently free of the New Age spirituality that clogs so much self-help literature. He's Ayn Randian. He survived because of his own strength, not divine intervention. The only god he worships is the god of the self. Unfortunately, he worships it all too much. Pelzer is unspeakably self-congratulatory: "I'm the real deal." He reminds readers of every award: "Here I was, an Outstanding Young Person of the World." His Web site is headlined: "Author-Samaritan-Activist." His other characters constantly tongue-bathe him: "You're the most inspirational person I know." His book "is one in a million." Everyone else speaks in "ain'ts" and dialect, but Dave always sounds like a Rhodes scholar. He exaggerates his accomplishments. He refueled planes during the Panama invasion and the Gulf War: This he describes as "play[ing] a major role in operations Just Cause, Desert Shield, and Desert Storm." He calls himself a "Pulitzer nominee," though he wasn't a Pulitzer winner or "nominated finalist." Someone may have submitted his book for the award, but by that standard, if you mailed one of my articles to the Pulitzer judges, I would be a "Pulitzer nominee" too.

According to a damning *New York Times* story, Pelzer seems to have boosted sales of his own book—and perhaps even kept it on the list—by buying it himself. But even the list isn't welcoming to Pelzer anymore. His books have mostly dropped off it in the last couple of years—perhaps because the public is exhausted with masochistic memoirs. Or it could be that—post-Frey—readers have less patience with books that strain belief. More likely Pelzer himself is out of gas. He has no more gory stories to tell. His most recent—and least successful—memoir is cheery and inspirational, lacking the blood and tears of the first three. Pelzer's rich. He's happily married. He's a loving father. He's learned to deal with the memory of abuse. He's a confessional author with nothing left to confess. He really is just A Man Named Dave, and—take it from another man named Dave—that's rarely enough to sell a million copies of anything.

Bill O'Reilly

It takes a snob to know one.

BY MICHAEL KINSLEY

DO YOU BELIEVE THIS STORY?

Bill O'Reilly, the Fox News talk show host, is in the capital for the Bush inauguration. He is invited to a fancy dinner party. Reluctantly, he accepts, although it is not his kind of thing. According to *Newsweek*, "O'Reilly said he could feel the socialites and bigwigs 'measuring' him. 'They're saying, "What's he doing here?" One couple even got up to leave,' O'Reilly later recalled."

Two people left a Washington dinner party rather than share a table with a prole like Bill O'Reilly? Although I wasn't there, I state baldly: It never happened. That kind of snobbery barely exists in America. (The *Wall Street Journal* recently had a front-page feature on country clubs that exclude Jews, treating the matter—correctly—as an odd cultural cul-de-sac, like a town where everyone plays hopscotch or a Web site devoted to whistling.) Certainly, traditional snobbery cannot hope to compete with today's most powerful social ordering principle: celebrity. O'Reilly, as he himself has been known to admit, has the most popular news show on cable. His books are huge best sellers. When he appears at an "A-list" (*Newsweek*'s label) social function, nobody wonders, "What's he doing here?"

Yet O'Reilly, like many other people, clings to the fantasy that he is a stiff among the swells. He plays this chord repeatedly in his book *The O'Reilly Factor*, a potpourri of anecdotes and opinions about life in general and his in particular. He had a very strange experience as a graduate student at Harvard's Kennedy School of Government (which let the likes of Bill O'Reilly through its ivy-covered gates, he is careful to note, "in an effort to bring all sorts of people together"). Other Kennedy School students, he says, insisted on being called by three names, none of which could be "Vinny, Stevie, or Serge." Their "clothing was understated but top quality . . . and their rooms hinted of exotic vacations and sprawling family property. Winter skiing in Grindelwald? No problem." They tried to be nice, but Bill was nevertheless humiliated, in a Thai restaurant, to be "the only one who didn't know how to order my meal in Thai."

I should explain this last one to those who may not have been aware that Thai is the lingua franca of the American WASP upper class. The explanation is simple. American Jewish parents only one or two generations off the boat often spoke in Yiddish when they didn't want their children to understand. Italian-Americans used Italian, and so on. But WASPs only had English. (They tried Latin, but tended to forget the declensions after the second martini.) So they adopted Thai, which they use in front of the servants and the O'Reillys of the world as well. (At least it sounds like Thai after the second martini.) When they turn 18, upper-class children attend a secret Thai language school, disguised as a ski resort, in Grindelwald.

The notion that the Kennedy School of Government, populated by swells out of P.G. Wodehouse, reached out to O'Reilly, a poor orphan out of Dickens, as representing the opposite pole of the human experience, would be remarkable enough. But O'Reilly's chapter on "The Class Factor" (Chapter 1, luckily for me) contains some puzzling counterevidence. "I'm working-class Irish American Bill O'Reilly . . . pretty far down the social totem pole," he says. Growing up in the 1960s, he watched his father "exhausting himself commuting from Levittown" to work as an accountant for an oil company. Dad "never made more than $35,000"—which would be $100,000 or more in today's money.

Oh, the shame of it! O'Reilly has been downward social climbing. He is actually—and I wish I could say this in Thai, to avoid humiliating him with the children—m-i-d-d-l-e c-l-a-s-s. He apparently regards that status with just as much horror as do the toffs of his fevered imagination.

Why fake a humble background? Partly for business reasons: Joe Sixpack versus the elitists is a good posture for any talk show host, especially one on Fox. Partly out of vanity: It makes the climb to your current perch more impressive. Partly for political reasons: Under our system, even conservatives need some plausible theory to qualify for victim status, from which all blessings flow. But mainly out of sheer snobbery. And it's the only kind of snobbery with any real power in America today: reverse snobbery. Bill O'Reilly pretends (or maybe sincerely imagines) that he feels the sting of status from above. But he unintentionally reveals that he actually fears it more from below. Like most of us.

This is not a terrible thing. Reverse snobbery, unlike the traditional kind, is a tribute to democracy—it's egalitarianism overshooting the mark. And it is a countervailing social force against growing economic disparity. But when you're faking it, if you're not careful, reverse snobbery can look a lot like the traditional kind. Bill O'Reilly told *Newsweek* he would never patronize a Starbucks, because he prefers a Long Island coffee shop "where cops and firemen hang out." Guess what, Bill! Cops and firemen like good coffee too! And they can afford it. Starbucks is one of the great democratizing institutions of our time. You'd know that if you went in there occasionally. You snob.

Contributor's Notes

Michael Crowley is a senior editor at the *New Republic*.

Dave Cullen has written for Salon.com, NPR, and the *New York Times* and is the author of the forthcoming book, *A Lasting Impression on the World: The Definitive Account of Columbine and its Aftermath*. He also maintains "The Columbine Navigator," the premier guide to the Columbine myths and media coverage, at www.davecullen.com.

Bryan Curtis is a *Slate* staff writer.

Andrew Ferguson is a senior editor at the *Weekly Standard*.

Frank Foer is the editor of the *New Republic*.

Michael Kinsley is *Slate*'s founding editor.

Josh Levin is a *Slate* assistant editor.

Michael Lind is a senior fellow at the New America Foundation. With Ted Halstead, he is the author of *The Radical Center: The Future of American Politics*. He is also the author of *Made in Texas: George W. Bush and the Southern Takeover of American Politics*.

Dahlia Lithwick is a *Slate* senior editor.

Field Maloney is on the editorial staff of *The New Yorker*.

Stephen Metcalf is *Slate*'s critic at large. He is working on a book about the 1980s.

Jill Hunter Pellettieri is *Slate*'s managing editor.

David Plotz is *Slate*'s deputy editor. He is the author of *The Genius Factory: The Curious History of the Nobel Prize Sperm Bank.*

Chris Suellentrop, a writer in Washington, D.C., is a former *Slate* staffer.

Jacob Weisberg is editor of *Slate* and co-author, with Robert E. Rubin, of *In an Uncertain World.*

Ben Yagoda is the author of *The Sound on the Page: Style and Voice in Writing*, and *If You Catch an Adjective, Kill It: The Parts of Speech, for Better and/or Worse.*